THE YOUNIVERSE

Gestalt Therapy, Non-Western Religions, and the Present Age

by

Jesse James Thomas, Ph.D.

PSYCHOLOGY AND CONSULTING ASSOCIATES PRESS
LA JOLLA, CALIFORNIA

COPYRIGHT © 1977

TO

MARY ALICE,
CARLA,
CLAUDIA,
LISA,
AND JESSICA

TABLE OF CONTENTS

PREFACE

The Youniverse may be a new name, but it is not a new reality. *As suggested in the name, it is any experience in which the line of distinction that usually separates you from what is around you disappears, where you and the universe become one.* Some know it best in the context of their work, some in sports, some in sexual activity, some in becoming absorbed in a work of art, some in the practice of meditation. Western psychology talks about it in terms of awareness, Eastern religions in terms of enlightenment. In a basic sense, it is impossible to talk about consciousness at all in any language without it.

This book deals with the Youniverse on two different levels: (1) on the level of understanding by *talking about* it, and (2) on the level of experience by *experimenting with* it by means of exercises.

On the level of understanding, the book is an effort to "get it together" concerning some of the confusion about Youniversal experiences, to weave together some of the loose ends: some artistic, some scientific and technological, some therapeutic, some religious. Sufism, a mystical offshoot from medieval Mohammedism, has many stories about getting things together, including the famous one about four men in the dark exploring an elephant, which none of them had ever seen before. They fall into a violent argument, because each of them has touched a different part of the elephant, so that his account disagrees completely with the others. One point of the story is that every one of them is right. He *has* experienced an elephant, he knows it, and he is right. Nobody is wrong as such. They do have their differences, but a difference can be a "difference of dependence." Parts of any whole are not only *different from* each other, they *depend on* each other. What the men in the dark fail to see is that their descriptions need each other just as much as the parts of the elephant need each other.

This book will eventually go the way of all partial descriptions. It will fade and disappear. In the meantime, however, it is a conscious effort to show how different ways of thinking can depend on each other. Confusion is always as interesting as it is frustrating. The only problem is that it is not yet clear how the confusing parts depend on each other.

Consider the three parts of this book in the same way. In some respects they may appear to contradict each other. But here again the differences may be differences of dependence. They may simply need each other. This is pointed out specifically in a few instances, but no effort is made to "resolve" all the differences. Each section has its use, and each, hopefully, can enrich rather than diminish the others. The purpose of this book is not to declare some kind of final and absolute truth. It is simply to provide a context for growth.

This book is admittedly a theoretical book and is designed for people who like to think, to play with ideas. It is for people with a certain amount of intellectual curiosity, who want to understand themselves in terms of the age in which they live. It is a tract for the times. But because growth takes place in experience as well as understanding, exercises are found alongside the "theory." As indicated in the text, some of the exercises are adapted from various therapeutic and religious traditions. Others are original to this book. You may wish to read the book and then go back and do the exercises or you may wish to do them as you read. In any event, don't just read about them. Try them and see what happens in and for yourself.

Do not, however, set up a rigid program of exercises for yourself. Self-discipline is a far more dangerous activity than most people realize. Self-discipline consists in pushing yourself to do what you don't really want to do, and that can be dangerous. If you discover in *any* set of psychological or meditative exercises that you are in a frightening place where you have lost your bearings, a place where you may even fear for your sanity, it may be because you are either pushing yourself or allowing yourself to be pushed into something before you are ready for it. This is the origin of most of the "casualties" of the human potential movement. Compulsive pushing and pulling on oneself will be discussed at length later in the book, but it should be made clear at the outset that the best way to approach these exercises is by getting in touch with your own needs in relation to them. What you need at any given moment is far more important than how "well" you are doing your exercises.

It is therefore left to you the reader to assume responsibility for what use you will make of the exercises. Most of them you will find simple, easy, and enjoyable. They will open up interesting new dimensions for you to explore and inhabit. In the unlikely event, however, that you begin to feel any severe strain on your system, the best remedy is to stop and wait until you feel *ready* to proceed. Some new dimensions are, to be sure, unavoidably difficult and painful on first contact, but there is a great difference between proceeding into such areas when you are ready to do so and pushing yourself into them when you are not ready. So try to get some feeling for that difference as you move through the book. Discover the flow that you are and learn to go with that flow.

The purpose of the exercises is to provide experiences that you will find useful and enjoyable depending on who you are and where you happen to be at that moment. Some exercises you may wish to do many times; others you may wish to do only once if at all. Some you will have done before; others will be completely new. The focus, in any case, is on the *experience,* not on the *program.* Productive experiences reinforce themselves. They do not need to be reinforced by self-discipline. If you do exercises in a rigid, programmatic way rather than in terms of your own needs and readiness, you constantly interfere with yourself and your own processes. The exercises will then result in a continual internal struggle in which the needs will usually win out sooner or later against the program anyway. However, if you concentrate on what you are *ready* to do rather than what you *should* do, then all of your energies can be put to use. There is nothing troublesome left over and nothing is lost. It then becomes possible to move one further step and realize that when all of your energies are being used, *all* of life can become the exercise. You cannot stop learning and growing no matter what you do. You don't have to take time out for exercises, as if the exercises are something different from everyday living. At that point exercises in the usual sense become unimportant. You transcend the need for exercises by becoming one. Then you can throw away this book and these exercises. You have it (you) together.

One last word concerning the illustrations in the book, which are petroglyphs (rock art) done by American Indians. These petroglyphs are chosen carefully, but they are not "explained" in any detail in the text because they speak for themselves nonverbally and enter into their own kind of dialogue with the text. Petroglyphs are found in hundreds of locations in this country. It is tragic that so many of them have been destroyed, defaced, or removed by guns, spray paint, and high speed drills. Many well intentioned people have carried them away for decorative use in their homes. Unfortunately, even with the help of existing and pending legislation, it is virtually impossible to police and protect more than a few sites. It would be still more tragic, however, if a single one of the petroglyphs shown in this book were to suffer similar destruction, and for that reason their locations are not given.

Jesse James Thomas, Ph.D.
Gestalt Institute of San Diego

PRELUDE

It is the middle of the night. You are sitting in a forest near a large rock covered with Indian inscriptions. You have been fasting there for three days, your only nourishment water from the stream that flows a few feet from the rock. Huge trees surround you. It is very dark, and for a long time it is very still.

Then in the distance you hear the rumble of the one whom the Indians call the Thunderbird, who flies toward you as clouds fill the sky. You are afraid now and want to flee but are transfixed by what is happening. Lightning begins to flash, dimly at first, then more brightly as the Thunderbird flies still closer. Time and again the forest lights up in pale white light. What a strange thing, you think, light that makes a sound!

A shudder comes over you. You notice that the flashes seem to stay on for an abnormally long time. That's not the way it's supposed to happen. It's as if an enormous cosmic movie is beginning to flicker. Now the light is staying on all the time and so is the thunder, which becomes a strange slow-motion rumble across the sky. You glance at the rock and particularly notice a large spiral inscription that glows with a strange iridescence. As you look, it seems to draw you into itself. You get up and with difficulty walk over to it.

As you do, it begins to twist, to turn, and to grow.

The rumble becomes that of an earthquake or an avalanche. You are terrified. Everything around you begins to stretch out of shape and get sucked into the spin as you, too, lose your hold and are caught in the swirl. It is futile to struggle against the invisible power that pulls you, so you finally let yourself go and fall, slowly spinning toward the brilliant white light at the center. The thunder, which is all around you now, becomes a gigantic whisper, which says: "DO NOT BE AFRAID. . . . I AM YOU."

PART I
THE FIRST YOUNIVERSAL:
The Youniverse is enstatic (indwelling).
You are the Youniverse and the Youniverse is you.
The Youniverse is the _You_niverse.

No clear lines exist between you and the universe. You part-icipate in the universe. You are it and it is you. So you and the universe are not two but one, as experience is one. Therefore only one word is fundamental, has meaning in itself, and that is the Youniverse. In isolation you make no sense. You do not exist. Together with the universe you make one sense. You are an indwelling (an *enstasis*) of the universe. *Enstasis* is the opposite of *ecstasis*: it is a coming into oneself rather than a being beside oneself or outside of oneself. The Youniverse is enstatic because the whole of the universe is found in the whole of you. Separation is an illusion. The Youniverse is the _You_niverse.

Holography is the technique of projecting three dimensional images (rather than the two dimensional images of "normal" photography or even so-called 3-D photography that gives the stereoscopic illusion of three dimensions) by using laser beams, beam splitters, camera, and photographic plates. While the exposed and developed photographic plate is only a strange jumble of interference patterns when viewed in ordinary light, the light of a laser beam opens up a marvelous, three dimensional world on the other side of it. It is even possible to view the image from different angles as you move from side to side and see different parts or sides of the image, just as you would if it were really there. Very complicated holographs have been created where it is possible to walk all the way around the image and see it from all sides. Yet it is impossible to touch the image, because physically, at least in the way that it appears, it is not there.

The image on the holographic plate is indistinguishable when viewed in ordinary light because, strange as it may seem, every point on the image is literally spread all over the plate. As a result of this, if one cuts the original plate into several parts, each part can be used to project a full image. Thus the mystery of the holograph. The whole is found in all the parts.

The whole of you is found in all your parts just as the whole is found in all the parts of the holographic plate. Every part, physical or psychological, is *you.* And the whole of the universe is found in you *as* a part in the same way. You are not separate; you are spread out into the universe. It is as if your identity is not just the separate you whom you see when you look in a mirror but the you who is known by and resides in the minds and lives of all your acquaintances. All people and all things are much more connected than appears. Separation is an illusion. A holograph is a holygraph.

Holographic reality is similar in certain respects to the number one. One stands for unit within a whole (in relation to a number larger than one) and also as a whole in itself (in relation to a number smaller than one). It is at once divider and dividend. So also with you. You function in the universe as a holograph within a holograph. You are unit and whole at the same time. It is like self and Self in Hindu thought, consciousness and Consciousness. So with all the microcosms and macrocosms of the universe. Nothing is found outside that is not found inside. It is said that the mass of particles in an atom is proportionally equal to the mass of celestial bodies in space. Perhaps one could communicate as easily with a virus on earth as with a creature from outer space.

The Youniversal holograph is everywhere. If *anything* is understood, *everything* is understood. The whole is found in all the parts. The complicated Irish novelist James Joyce was one of the first Westerners to experience this deeply. His novel *Ulysses* (1922) is the first holographic work of art. Nothing has clear edges. Every chapter is found in some miniature version in every other chapter. Meaning is spread over the whole of the book in such a way that whoever understands anything, even the painting on Bloom's bedroom wall, understands everything. If this is true of *Ulysses,* it is even more true of his later work *Finnegans Wake* (1939), the most elaborate and complex cultural holograph ever created, nothing standing in isolation, the whole meaning found in the tiniest part. Nothing is insignificant. Nothing stands by itself. Everything is part of everything else. In a holograph the possibilities of meaning are not added but multiplied. If a (two dimensional) picture is worth a thousand words, how much is a holograph worth?

8

This is the age of holology rather than theology. What is the relation of the part to the whole? That question dominates the age. What does it mean to participate? What is my own internal unity and externally that of me with the universe? It is the Youniversal question.

It is not a supernatural God looking down from his supernatural heaven but "nature," anything and everything that happens around you, that provides the clearest model of what you are and can be. Nature is full of illusions and deceptions, to be sure, but she herself is quite capable of removing her veils and showing herself. Truth is not transcendent so much as immanent. The only thing that makes sense of everything is the Here and Now, not something or someone from somewhere else, some other order of existence. Everything that anyone needs to know arises from the present. In fact, that is *what* one needs to know.

In the East time itself is understood in a holographic way. Every moment is spread over every other moment. The smallest event contains every other event and the whole of eternity itself. Time is more an overlay than a progression of events. When one understands this, time and space in the usual Western sense disappear and the eternal Here and Now appears. In *Finnegans Wake* the last page of the book is the page just before the first page. Astral projection (either in time or space) is available in principle at any moment, for every time and every place are here all the time anyway. So all one needs to do is to go into the center of the Present to find anywhere and anywhen. The Youniverse is enstatic. Eternity lives in you, although you may not notice it. That is what is meant by the *You*niverse. So holo, who are you?

KNOWING THE _YOU_ NIVERSE

You (singular) are more than the sum of your parts.
You are not just arms and legs, head and torso. You are
a holographic whole. And your wholeness is found in the
smallest part of you and what you do. Wholeness is
inevitable; it cannot be escaped. It is present whether you
are conscious of it or not.

Wherever people have tried to draw lines, they have
failed. In earlier Western thought the "body" was seen
as separate from the "mind," continually dragging it down,
blocking it from the achievement of truth, goodness, and
happiness. The Greeks saw it as a limitation, the Christians
as a temptation. In either case it was as if the mind (or
spirit) and body were very different things. Nowadays they
are not all that separable. In one sense the body may even
be considered as a picture of the mind. Whatever is
happening in one is happening in the other. Your psychological make-up is not just located in your mind; it is located
all over you. Quite literally you carry the burden of your
moral standards on your back. Your fear is the tightness
in your chest. The ache in your stomach is the ache of
your mind trying to "digest" what it does not want. If
you are having trouble solving a problem with your mind,
your body is having the same problem. Your body is always
an indicator of what is wrong and what needs to be done,
not just with your body but with your mind as well.

Learning and therapy can be approached from the side
of the body as easily as, perhaps easier than, from the
mind. At this moment your body is performing countless
incredibly complex operations, creating antibodies, resisting
diseases, balancing systems and subsystems with unbe-

11

lievable delicacy, sensitive to the most minute changes in the environment. As any practitioner of yoga, bioenergetics, or structural integration (popularly known as Rolfing) can tell you, the most direct route to the therapeutic release of painful memories is often through some bodily action. The legendary Irish hero Cuchulain discovers that he has killed his own son and in his grief literally wages a battle with the tide. This may seem futile, but it is more body-wise than may appear. It certainly makes much more sense than "sitting around" and trying to justify the act on a purely intellectual level. Body languages tend to be more honest and direct (unless tampered with self-consciously) than verbal-intellectual languages. Your eyes, hands, and the kind of space that you occupy when you speak often say far more than your words. Even the manner in which you use your mouth or the sound of your voice may be saying more than your words.

As an exercise, go without speaking for a significant period of time and see what you notice. Holy men in the East sometimes do this for years at a time. Among other things it gives special significance to the first words that you speak at the end of the silence. If you cannot be completely silent without calling undue attention to yourself, at least keep your words to an absolute minimum so that you can watch both yourself and others. The most intimate secrets become obvious when you learn to look for them. Watch the posture, the gestures, the facial expressions. Ignore the words. The most interesting languages exist between people that are spoken and understood on a completely nonverbal and unconscious level. Perhaps the "universal" language that the future holds will be nothing like Esperanto or any other verbal language. If the parts of the body can communicate with each other by means of complex nonverbal signals, perhaps a similar thing can happen between people.

Who you *think* you are may be only a small part of who you really are. What you take to be the whole may only be a part. Your holographic qualities in this respect show up readily in your dreams. You are not just the protagonist, the "leading character," the self-conscious you of your dreams; you are all the other characters, even the objects and atmospheres, as well. It is the dream that is you, not just the character in the dream who bears your name. A basic procedure in Gestalt therapy is to act out the various parts of the dream, to get into the thoughts and feelings that go with those parts, to "be" the spider, the old house, the wall, or the bridge as well as the other people.

Do this with one of your dreams. Make a cast of all of the characters, animate or inanimate. Then, one at a time, become those parts. Actually experience yourself as the character; don't just think about it. With some parts you may want to act it out physically. In any case, see how it *feels* to be that part. Then see if you can accept that character as you. Do this with every person and object in the dream. You will discover that even what at first appear to be external, inadmissible parts are in some way yourself. If you find a part that you cannot accept no matter what you do, try it again at some later time. Don't be content with your initial rejection of it. Finally, become the whole of the dream. Experience all the actions and interactions that take place in the dream as taking place in yourself. Make some statements about the dream as a whole and see if they are statements about you. Own the processes that take place in the dream as *your* processes.

You can deal with daydreams and fantasies in the same way. As a further exercise,[1] find a comfortable, quiet place

14

and either lie down or sit in a chair in your best daydreaming position. Let go of all the tightness that you feel in your body and relax. Imagine that you are walking through a forest. It makes no difference whether this is a real or imaginary forest. Simply look down inside yourself until you see a forest. You don't have to "invent" one. Just look for the one that is there already. When you find it, walk through it and experience it in every way that you can. Look at it, listen to it, and feel it.

After you have done that for a while, notice that there is a clearing in the trees ahead of you and that when you come out into the clearing, you discover a stream. Again, look for the stream that is already there. This stream offers several possibilities. You can sit down and look at it, you can cross it, you can walk along its banks upstream or downstream, or you can go wading or swimming in it. Choose one of these and do it for a while. Take your time. Surrender yourself to the experience. Stay for as long as you like. When you are ready to leave, take a last look back at the stream and then walk back through the forest to the point where you entered it, noticing anything that you may not have noticed when you walked the other direction. Keep walking until you feel that you are back where you started. Then wake up from your daydream.

Consider your daydream in the same way that you did your night dream in the previous exercise. One at a time become the things that you saw. Become one of the trees, animals, birds, flowers, the stream, the weather, the sun shining in the sky. Take your time. Don't rush. Again, don't just think *about* each one; experience yourself *as* it. Make a one sentence description of yourself in the role and then see if it fits you as the one who had the

15

daydream. It may be a resourceful part of you, it may be a troublesome part of you, but it is always you.

In Gestalt therapy such an exercise falls under the heading of "owning" responsibility for oneself as opposed to "disowning" responsibility. Disowning is similar to what Sartre calls "bad faith."[2] It is a lie to oneself, a kind of double mindedness. It is a separation in the oneness, a not being "together." To own responsibility is a difficult but necessary process. It is difficult, for example, for a child to acknowledge that the hands that he fantasizes reaching over the headboard of his bed to grab and strangle him in the night are, when he keeps his eyes open and looks, his own hands. But until he does, the power of those hands will never be his own.

The unity of the self is a marvelous and inescapable phenomenon. Even the worst double mindedness leaves you with the realization that you are singular, not plural. The worst confusion leaves you with the realization that *you* are confused; hence the confusion is always unified by the one who *is* confused. It is as if the single cell from which everyone came is still present in the many cells, as if the multiplication of cells in the growth process is as much a division as it is a multiplication. Is it a matter of one cell becoming many, or of one cell gaining many parts? In any case there still remains something of the original cell in every new cell that grows. Even the tiniest, most insignificant cell in the body still has something of the original cell in it.

In his book *The Parable of the Beast* Bleibtrau speculates about the way in which traces of the whole organic process are found in individual organisms. He calls this the "molecular memory." "For each of us then, as we pass from nonbeing into being, there moves with us like the tail of a comet, . . . remembrances of infinitudes of time-past. This is meaning of a strange sort—memory manifested in biochemical energy."[3] Who knows what is available in a single cell? Perhaps from a single one of your cells, the whole of you could be reconstructed. And since your original cell also belonged to your parent whose original cell belonged to his or her parent and so on, perhaps the whole history of the human race could be reconstructed. Who knows what is happening in the unconsciousness of an embryo or an infant? How fanciful is the star-child in *2001: Space Odyssey*?

17

Scientists are now much interested in biorhythms, the pulsations of life and the universe. The universe is full of strange cycles and cycles within cycles. Women menstruate according to a more or less lunar cycle. Sandcrabs turn from red to black depending on whether it is day or night and show ability to do this when completely removed from sunlight for long periods of time. Moreover, they adapt to different latitudes and therefore different daylight hours without ever seeing daylight on the way to or in the new location. How they do this is a matter of speculation. What is important is that the universe is full of these rhythms and that they often seem to contain each other, much as Thoreau points out how the cycle of the year takes place every day on a small scale.

Things do not just happen once; they are happening all the time. It is as if the timeless (present) importance of any event is spread out holographically through the moments of time, perhaps as a reminder to those who find it easy to forget. Recurring dreams are important to the extent that they recur. Every recurrence is a reminder. For Joseph Conrad in his novelette *The Heart of Darkness* (1902) the beating of the drums along the Congo becomes the beating of a heart that is somehow responsible for the flow of the river itself. The beating is both a pulse and a message. So all the rhythms and cycles are like the pulsations of the Youniversal heart, pumping the same life, the same energy everywhere within the system. So, perhaps, they are also messages, reminders that it is from that pulse that consciousness itself emerges.

In the end there is (holographically) only one time and only one place, the Here and Now. One of the basic Gestalt exercises is to begin every sentence with the phrase "Here and now I am aware . . ." and follow it with whatever your present awareness happens to be. This exercise will appear several times in this book, each time with a somewhat different emphasis. For now simply notice how many times your attention drifts away from the present and into some other place or time, past or future. There is certainly nothing wrong with the past or future as such, so long as they do not interfere with the present and attending to present problems and enjoyments. But that is often exactly what happens. If you are too busy anticipating (or fearing) what will happen next, you cannot enjoy the present.

Do not, however, keep yourself from drifting away from the present. And try not to get lost in explanations as to *why* you drift away. Thinking too much can be another way of losing the present. Just watch yourself drifting away and notice what happens when you do. Also notice what happens when you come back. See how much or how little time you spend in the present and how it feels when you do.

According to Gestalt therapy all you need to do is to stay aware of what you *are* doing and the corrective process will take care of itself. Here and Now is the only medicine that you need. Failure to solve a psychological problem is not so much a matter of needing some internal resources that are *not* there as it is ignoring (for various reasons that will be dealt with later) resources that *are.* You don't have to force yourself to do anything. You don't have to solve your problems *for* you, as if you stand above yourself and manipulate yourself by pulling various strings. Change takes place spontaneously, without coercion, from within the Here and Now.

Ram Dass, the former Harvard professor and psychedelic adventurer Richard Alpert turned Hindu mystic, also has an exercise that helps to focus on the Here and Now.[4] You simply ask yourself often: "Where are you and what time is it?" and then answer: "Here and Now." Even post little signs around the house with the question printed on them, so that you won't always be expecting it. One point to the exercise is to realize that every time that you say "Here and Now," it is the same Here and Now that it was last time that you said it or will say it next time. It's always Here and Now. And when you realize that, you can live in it more easily. After all, as Ram Dass points out, you can't get away from it anyway. No matter how you try, you can't get out of Here. Everywhere you go, it's always Here for you. And no matter how long you take to get there, it's always Now. You cannot escape the Youniversal holograph. That's all there is. There is only one time and only one place. It is like the Zen question: "What does a flower look like before it blooms?" The answer is: "What a beautiful flower it is." You do not have to "go" anywhere in order to get into the Youniverse. The Youniverse is the _You_niverse. The Youniverse is Here and Now, and Here and Now is who you are.

DOING THE _YOU_ NIVERSE

As you participate in the Youniversal holograph, there is no point that is you in any isolated sense. The whole is found anywhere and everywhere. The points are spread over the whole just as the whole is found at every point. The clearcut distinction that seems to exist between you and what is around you is illusory. This is as much the insight of Western science and technology as it is of the non-Western religions. Nothing can be treated as isolated or separate. Human identity is spread out far beyond the boundaries of the body. Your skin does not enclose you. Marshall McLuhan has shown, for example, how media are your extensions,[5] that television is an extension of your eyes just as the automobile is an extension of your legs and that these extensions are as much a part of your perceptual apparatus as any of your organs. In a real sense your television set and your automobile _are_ you.

Your edges are much less distinct than you may suppose. Like a moebius strip in which one end of the strip is twisted and pasted back onto the other end, the distinction between outside and inside begins to fade. If you trace your finger along the surface, you will notice a continuous flowing from inside to outside and back inside again and so on _ad infinitum._ The inside and outside become one another. So it is with many such distinctions in our time. Inside and outside, subject and object, here and there: they all approach reversibility.

Consider how people "out there" enter into you and become part of you just as you do of them. You carry them around with you as part of you wherever you go, as they do you. You not only act *on* each other, you act *in* each other. What all is involved when W. H. Auden says in his dedicatory poem to William Butler Yeats when describing the day that Yeats died that: "It was his last afternoon as himself, he became his admirers"? Or consider the mysteries of the obscure statement: "Ontogeny (development of the individual organism) recapitulates phylogeny (development of the related group of organisms)." You may wake up some morning and discover that you *are* the history of the world.

When two people are in love, do they not become real to the extent that they cease to be particular individuals and become not two people but one? Is there such a thing as a medium, someone who ceases to be him or herself and becomes someone else? Is it not at least conceivable, given the "selflessness" of some holy men, that they constitute a single holy man rather than individual holy men. Perhaps a holy man can look at those around him in the same way that you can look at your own hand.

So the distinctions between you and what is around you continue to fade. You are not only what you eat, you are everything that is around you. Even when you die, perhaps it is not so much a matter of *disappearing from* the universe as it is *becoming* it. It is not as if you simply vanish into thin air or as if you reappear in some other place (heaven, hell, or whatever). There is only one place and only one time. You never "leave" the Youniverse.

In *Journey to Ixtlan* the Yaqui Indian medicine man Don Juan instructs his apprentice Carlos to talk to the plants around him in the desert, to realize that he is no more important than they, that in fact he can learn much from them.[6] Learn to talk with plants, even if it does seem silly. Are you afraid to look ridiculous in your own eyes? Talk to them aloud, so that the whole of you is involved, not just your mind, and so that you don't make a merely internal dialogue of it. Don Juan tells Carlos to talk to them in a loud voice. But also listen. Listen with your whole self. Listen with your eyes, ears, nose, and skin. Be careful not just to listen for words and ideas that the plants may express to you. Listen for feelings and moods. How does the plant *feel* to you?

The world is full of music. As the experimental composer John Cage tells us, what is usually called "music" is only for the purpose of calling our attention to the music that is around us all the time. Every sound is music, from the wheels of the train clicking on the track to the telephone ringing or the baby crying. Cage incorporates all of these sounds into his compositions. Listen to the music of the Youniverse. The world is talking to you all the time. William Burroughs has developed the same notion into a literary form. His later novels are elaborate collages of excerpts from his own earlier work, newspaper articles and advertisements, radio messages, road signs, conversations heard in passing, etc. All of these are juxtaposed in such a way as to allow the world to speak to the reader in the same way that Cage's music does. According to Burroughs the world is filled with secret instructions that can only be understood by an authentic agent of the Nova Police (whom Burroughs sets against the Nova Mob and the addictions

26

that they push on free men). Like the shaman (the "medicine man" in primitive hunting societies), he becomes skilled in hearing messages that are there all the time but that most people miss. The whole can be discovered in some of the most unlikely places.

Maya, the cosmic illusion according to Eastern religion, is the illusion of separation. *Maya* is the opposite of the Youniverse. Separated man is the one who lives in the illusion that he is "master" of his environment. "Multiply and subdue the earth." He never sees that in defeating his environment, he defeats himself. At the same time that Alexander "the Great" was destroying his enemies, he was destroying himself. Whatever is happening on the outside is happening on the inside. One possibility is separation, the other is unity, and real unity cannot be a purely internal process. It is inevitably an external one as well.

An exercise that helps to get in touch with this unity is what in the East is called a *mantram.* The most basic mantram is the untranslatable Sanskrit syllable OM (or AUM). It cannot be reduced to anything simpler or other than itself. Nor is there any distinction between its form and its content, its sound and its meaning. It *is* its own meaning. It is what it signifies. Any translation into English therefore loses this unity. The closest that it is possible to come is simply "the whole." It means and *is* the Self that is all selves. OM is the sound of the Youniverse.

Find a comfortable place and a comfortable position. You can sit cross-legged, on your knees with your weight resting back on your calves or ankles, or in a chair. You can even stand up or lie down flat on your back, except that you may get tired in the former or fall asleep too easily in the latter position. Another possibility is to lie on your back and keep your knees raised, so that in case you begin to fall asleep, your legs will drop and wake you up. Whatever position you choose, it is better to keep your spine as straight as possible. It also helps to breathe

28

as deeply and easily as possible.

According to some interpretations, the mantram should be pronounced in three parts, gradually modulating from "ah" to "oh" to "oom-m-m." Imagine that the sound is an opening, a relaxation that begins at the back of the throat and works its way forward to the lips and nostrils with the "m-m-m" sound at the end. One way to understand the mantram is that it is the sound that is *all* sounds, that it is, as it were, the original holographic sound. So imagine, particularly in the first part ("ah"), that you are opening yourself to this something that is everything. Then listen to the way in which, as the sound dies away at the end, the holograph fades back into the world that it represents. It is not there any longer, and yet it is.

Learn to play with OM. Play with the volume, duration, pitch, even your facial expression as you say it. Allow the mantram to say or sing itself in whatever way it pleases. Practice it if you can until it begins to sound strange to your ears and you begin to wonder whether you are making the sound or it is making you. At that moment maker and made become the same thing. You become the sound and it becomes you. From OM you may wish to go on to other mantrams, such as OM MANI PADME HUM. Again, don't worry about what it means, at least for the moment. Simply know that it is the sound of the Youniverse. Concentrate for now especially on the first syllable, OM. The other syllables will be emphasized in later exercises.

Unfortunately, sacred sounds are virtually unknown in the Western world. One modern exception is the 100 letter, holographic sound of the thunder in Joyce's *Finnegans Wake:* bababadalgharaghtakamminarronnkonnbronntonnerronntuonnthunntrovarrhounawnskawntoohoohoord-

29

enenthurnuk![7] Joyce gives no indication that it is to be sung as a mantram, but he clearly considered it to be the sound that is all sounds, the sound from which every sound comes, using the theory that man first began to talk in imitation of the sound of thunder, or in terms of the Prelude of this book, the Thunderbird.

As an experiment, try meditating on the buzzing or ringing sound that you hear in your ears. If you have not already noticed this sound, it may take some time to locate. When you do locate it, stay with it for as long as you can, but feel free to leave it when you want and then keep coming back to it every time that you think of it again. Like OM, the ringing sound in your ears is a fundamental sound. Listen to it as if all your thoughts come from it and return into it. There are, of course, many possible sounds to use for this kind of exercise. There is *no* sound that is not the sound of the Youniverse. Holiness is wholiness.

The following exercise requires that you have a partner, someone whom you are not afraid to trust. It is a variation on a meditation used in parts of the East and at the Arica schools in the West. Sit facing your partner with your faces no more than a foot apart and gaze into each other's eyes. Focus on the area between the eyes or slightly higher on the forehead, in the place of the "third eye" of Eastern tradition. Keep your gaze relaxed so that you can pay general attention to the whole of the other person's face. Even throw your eyes somewhat out of focus if you like. However, keep your eyes more or less in one place. Do not let them wander around once you get settled. And try not to blink them any more than necessary.

Beyond this there is nothing that you need to do. Just go with the experience so long as you do not move and interfere with the other person's experience. Continue the exercise for several minutes. Then stop and converse with each other about your experience. Of all the meditation exercises this is the one most likely to get significant results immediately. After this it is much easier to contemplate candle flames or navels or the end of your nose. You may be surprised not only at the visual effects but at the overlap between your experiences. It may be an insight into each other's problems, an unconscious sharing of a fantasy, even a momentary loss of your individual identities.

The usual distinction between subject and object disappears as the Youniversal Consciousness appears. If you (plural) consider who you are, you realize that you (plural) are you (singular). This is the meaning of love, or what in the novelist Kurt Vonnegut's language might be called the Karassable Bond. How can one man murder another when it is himself that he is murdering? One of religionist

John Blofeld's lama teachers of Tibetan Buddhism summed up Tantric attitude in three injunctions: "Recognize everything around you as Nirvana (blissful union); hear all sounds as mantra; see all beings as Buddhas."[8] This is the meaning of Youniversal love: surrender yourself to Yourself. It is at nobody's expense; it is for the enrichment of all. You cannot give something to someone else without giving it to yourself if the inside and outside are really one. It is a process in which giving and receiving, selfishness and unselfishness lose their meaning. It is a "coming together." You (plural) become you (singular). Love is the _You_niversal virtue.

ENJOYING THE _YOU_NIVERSE

The Youniverse is filled with special objects and events that join things together. Each of these "symbols" operates holographically. The whole is found in the part. The most intense of these are sacred words, places, objects, and events, all of which have extraordinary and awesome power to give meaning, to transform your relationship to what is around you. The less intense are what is usually called "culture." Every work of art, every language, every corporate act, even every thought that you have, every word that you speak, is a marvelous holographing, a Youniversalizing of the world.

Primitives understand sacred objects to be special and at the same time universal. A sacred object may look like other objects, but it is somehow inhabited by eternity itself. To possess such an object and manipulate it properly is to possess and manipulate (holographically) the reality in which it participates. This is the origin of magic and religion. "Hierophanies (manifestations of the sacred) have the peculiarity of seeking to reveal the sacred in its totality, even if the human beings in whose consciousness the sacred shows itself fasten upon only one aspect or one small part of it. In the most elementary hierophany _everything is declared._"[9] A hierophany is therefore a "wholy" experience.

Remember a moment when a cold chill ran up your spine, when you saw a rainbow, a flag, a person of national importance, a dark forest at night, or anything else that you knew at the time was not just another object or event like those around it but one invested with power and meaning that was out of the ordinary. The world of the primitive

33

is peopled with animals that are not simply animals, trees that are not simply trees, rocks that are not simply rocks. Walking past a rock with a spiral inscription on it as if it were just another rock would be like your walking past a tornado as if it were just another wind.

As an exercise, begin locating places that are wholly places for you. Watch for such places to appear wherever you go, but don't try to "think out" where they should be. You will have trouble if you try consciously to put them there. As in other exercises, get a feeling for them. And remember that this is not the kind of exercise that can be done in a few minutes. You may get some surprises, because the places may be where you least suspect. The best places are often those that are the most difficult to locate.

Then whenever you need help, rest, insight, or perhaps a place to do the exercises in this book, go to one of these places and absorb its energy in the process. Feel the place. Some of them may be frightening at first until you grow accustomed to them. But the measure is always found in the energy, the power that you find there. As you learn to inhabit such places, they will reinvigorate you. You may discover them in the house where you live. You may discover them anywhere.

As a more advanced exercise of the same sort, go outside on a night when the sky is clear and lie down on your back so that you can see the stars. Look at the sky until you discover that your attention is drawn to a particular star; let the star show itself to you. Just watch them all until you notice one that feels right to you. Then focus all your attention on this star. Breathe as if you are breathing into the light of the star and are drawing your breath from it. Whisper "ah" softly as you breathe out and make the same sound as you breathe in. Relax your breathing as much as you can and also relax any other tension that you feel in your body. Breathe those tensions into the star and draw from it the openness and freedom of outer space. Beyond that, just watch without blinking and let the star do the rest. Do not wait merely for messages, however. The test is not necessarily whether you hear messages but whether you feel differently afterward.

One role of the shaman is to point out and, together with the tribe or clan, to celebrate the space or event where the sacred inhabits the earth. This is the origin of ritual, the holographic celebration that brings together the members of the tribe with each other as well as with the source of the wholy. This is where dance, story telling, and all the other arts begin. A particular thing becomes the whole thing, as in the Greek philosopher Aristotle's "concrete universal." How appropriate when a story begins: "Once upon a time . . ."

So the shaman is the prototype of all artists, the one who points to the extraordinary in the ordinary. As in the work of James Joyce, the event is no longer simply an event, the person no longer simply a person. Finnegan's fall from his ladder is the origin of the sound of thunder. It is also Adam's fall, Humpty Dumpty's fall, the fall of Ireland, and even the Wall Street Crash. So Finnegan's "Wake" is his awakening and that of everyone from Thor to Buddha. Similarly, H.C.E., one of many names given to Finnegan during the novel, is not just one man but every man (*H*ere *C*omes *E*verybody), a walking Youniversal community.

The shaman may be not only the embodier but also the embodied. He[10] is himself a meeting of the sacred and the profane. He is a particular and at the same time a universal man. Hence he often wears a special costume, has special responsibilities, and is given a special place in the life of the community. He speaks for it and acts for it. He stands for it. He is not only its unifier; he is its embodiment. He is an artist who becomes his art, a Youniversal man.

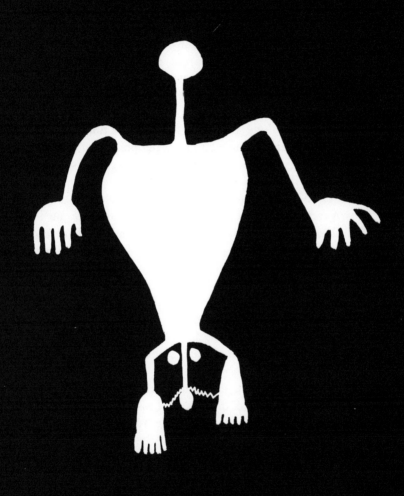

The Hindu equivalent of the shaman is the guru. He does not usually serve as artistic a function as the shaman, but in himself he specializes even more in the absorption of consciousness into Consciousness. The shaman normally keeps his own personality even when traveling in mystic worlds, but the guru eventually loses his and to the extent that he becomes a guru, the edges of his personality disappear and he becomes no one at all. "Living Lord of the Universe" hardly seems an appropriate designation in this respect. A guru is not the highest among men. He is the closest thing around to an absolute nobody.

It is strange to see so many people spending so much time, energy, and money chasing all over the world after gurus as if they were real somebodies. This pursuit of the exotic guru can often be taken as a picture of their own internal distance from themselves and the guru who is already within. Many people become adept at *putting* the truth in far distant places, which is only another method of self-alienation. While they are searching for truth in distant places, the truth may be following closely behind them, waiting in vain for them to turn around and look. Is it any wonder that such people so often come to disappointing conclusions?

Gurus in the external sense do, of course, exist, and some of them may be in distant places. Putting oneself in the hands of a guru, giving up "self-control," and obeying his every command may be necessary at certain points in one's spiritual pilgrimage in order to escape self-deceptive patterns that will otherwise only be reinforced. But one should be aware of the dangers of the "search" for such gurus. The wisdom of the East makes it clear that when an external guru is important it will all work out one way or another anyway. It is not so much a matter of your finding the guru as it is the guru's finding you (at the end of your "expectations").

If you wish to get in touch with the guru who is already inside you, find a wholy place where you can relax and daydream as in the earlier exercise. If necessary, do some of the meditation exercises already described. Then imagine that you are looking for a guru or otherwise wholy person (who may be either male or female) whom you wish to ask a question, a question that dominates your life at the present moment, not just a supposedly important question for which you have no real use anyway. When you have this question, take it with you as you imagine hiking across a hilly countryside toward the place where this wholy person is reported to be, which is just beyond the top of a ridge that you can see ahead of you.

As you climb that ridge, notice that it is a sunny day and enjoy the warmth of the sun as you climb, getting closer and closer to the top. Allow yourself plenty of time for this part of the trip. Don't get in a hurry. When you do get to the top, you look over the edge and see the wholy person sitting on a ledge gazing into a beautiful valley on the other side. When (s)he turns and recognizes you, walk over and sit down. When you feel ready, ask your question. Wait and watch carefully for the reply, which may not be in words. (S)he may reply by drawing something on the ground, by pointing to something in the valley, or by showing you something that (s)he holds in one hand. Stay until you feel that you have learned as much as you can or until (s)he lets you know that it is time to leave. Find an appropriate way to say goodbye, remembering that you can return whenever you are ready. Make your way back down the ridge and hike back across the hills to where you started. Then wake up.

A guru is as close to you as you are to yourself. If you know someone in the "exterior" world who can answer your questions or help you with your problems, so much the better, but if you don't, you always have a guru inside. Subsequent trips inside yourself can result in all kinds of interesting things. The guru whom you met on this trip may be replaced by others as time goes on. (S)he may send you on to other places. (S)he may also appear in the dreams that you have at night.

If you do have an external guru, you may discover that same guru on the inside. Fritz Perls, the originator of Gestalt therapy, was fond of telling people as they left his workshops that there was such a Fritz whom they could take with them, one who was inside them and knew more than he did about them anyway, and that this Fritz was always available. So in a perhaps deeper but similar way, the devotee always carries his or her guru somewhere inside. Many meditative exercises work on that supposition, including the one where you imagine the guru first sitting on your head in miniature form and then growing and descending into you and filling you up from the inside until you (plural) become you (singular). After all, you do contain the whole of the universe inside you, and that includes your guru. You are the _You_niverse.

PART II

THE SECOND YOUNIVERSAL:

The Youniverse is homeostatic.
You and the universe depend on each other.
The Youniverse is the Yo*u*niverse

Youniverse as a "new" word is formed by the overlapping of two "old" words. Nothing new is added except for the *relation between* them. The two old words are merely put in such a way that they depend on each other. The focus here is not so much on identity, of what they have in common (Part I), as it is on interdependence, on the balance or equilibrium (homeostasis) that takes place between them. So with you and the universe. In the end neither you nor the universe can be defined in yourselves. You can only be defined in terms of interdependence, of the interaction between you. The Youniverse is homeostatic.

On a scientific-technological level this is the age of "relativity." Physics since Einstein, field theory, cybernetics, the technology of electric circuitry, systems analysis, and ecology are some of the most obvious examples. Objects in themselves become unimportant; interactions become important. Every action is understood in terms of a network of reactions, restraints, feedback. Nothing happens by itself. It happens in context, in relation. Terms like symbiosis (interdependent living) and synergy (interdependent energy) have come into existence in order to describe what it is like for things to "happen together." It is as if the ground of being is the relation *between* things, the "interface" as it is sometimes called, rather than what things are in themselves. It is as if things have no *inherent* properties, as if the only basis for understanding anything is an understanding of what it is *not*.

In art this is the age of the multiple viewpoint, of the mosaic, the collage, the multi-media environment. The West has developed its own kind of artistic parallels to Chinese painting, where the subject of the painting is the space between the mountains as much as it is the mountains themselves. The focus is not on things themselves. It is on their interdependent parts or their interdependence with other things in the environment. The cubists painted the object from many different points of view at once so that the parts could inter-relate. The same thing is true of T. S. Eliot's early poetry, which so shook the foundations of twentieth century poetry, and the novels of James Joyce, which did much the same thing to the twentieth century novel. Again, the art is not in the object so much as in the relation.

The parts of a "system" depend on each other. That

is what makes a system: physical, psychological, political, industrial, ecological, or whatever. Even in relatively simple systems the parts cooperate with great complexity. A good place to look at this in a psychological perspective is in the area of dreaming. Not only is the dreamer found in all the parts of his dream, as indicated earlier, but those parts interact with each other. Anyone who thinks that (s)he can only do "one thing at a time" is well advised to look at what (s)he is doing all the time in a dream, where (s)he creates an entire cast, all of whom relate to each other continually and often in very complicated ways.

It is questionable whether anyone really has a "one-track" mind. The brain researcher Karl Pribram has proposed, for example, a "two-process" model for the operation of the nervous system itself. As he sees it, the neuron and the neural junction operate at least somewhat independently of each other.[1] Each process has its use, and although it is not clear how, they may even require each other in some way that is not yet understood. This is similar to many of the paradoxes of relativity theory in physics. The either/or mentality is being replaced by a both/and mentality. Human consciousness is like a Sufi story, many different levels with no obvious connection with each other operating at once in a strange kind of harmony. A Zen question asks what one's face looked like before one was born. Another question might be: What does one's interface look like now?

The way of homeostasis is to learn to balance in the "space between." The ancient Chinese religion Taoism and Zen Buddhism are especially aware of this space. As the *Tao te Ching,* the sacred book of the Taoists puts it:

> Thirty spokes share the wheel's hub;
> It is the center hole that makes it useful.
> Shape clay into a vessel;
> It is the space within that makes it useful.
> Cut doors and windows for a room;
> It is the holes which make it useful.
> Therefore profit comes from what is there;
> Usefulness from what is not there.[2]

Or as Suzuki, the famous authority on Zen Buddhism, explains the Mondo, or question and answer technique of Zen instruction: "Mondo, then, means mutuality, or co-responding. As long as the Originally Pure remains pure, that is, remains within itself and in itself and does not ask any question, there is no splitting, hence no answering, no mutuality, no 'participation.' When any question comes out at all, it sees itself, reflected in the form of 'the ten thousand things' in the mountains and the rivers and the great earth."[3]

Becoming aware of the "Originally Pure," or the "zero point" as Perls calls it, is what allows for corresponding (co-responding) or dialogue between the dualities. If all the parts, whether of an individual organism or a larger system, speak to and relate to each other, balance is possible. If not, the individual organism or larger system collapses into chaos and death. "Participation" is not just involvement in a larger whole: it is also the parts "in concert" with each other. It is point and counterpoint, the awesome and beautiful attempt to reach and maintain an elusive equilibrium (homeostasis). In its simplest form: if you don't eat and breathe, you die. Existence is interrelating. The Youniverse is the You_niverse.

KNOWING THE YOUNIVERSE

The Youniverse is the space between. What is there is not nearly so important as what is *not* there. You do not need to "get hold of yourself." You need to let go of yourself and get in touch with your *un*self. But how can you talk about what is not there to talk about? In one sense, however, there is nothing else that you *can* talk about. A fundamental quality of all physical and human systems is the "polar" relation. It is impossible to define anything apart from its opposite. All reality seems to have a "binary" base. Everything intelligible is on some continuum of opposites: on-off, positive-negative, hot-cold, good-bad, and so on *ad infinitum.* You yourself are an amazing collection or composite of such opposites—physical, emotional, intellectual, moral—all interacting with each other. It is the well known principle of the Yin and the Yang in Chinese thought. Opposites only *appear* to be irreconcilable. In fact they *require* each other. As Alan Watts puts it: "This essential duality and multiplicity of facts should be the clearest evidence of their interdependence and inseparability."[4] Every pair of opposites is a coupling. They belong together.

Only one side of the opposition may be apparent, but the other is always there. Pride and feelings of inferiority, for example, bring each other into existence. The secret of getting out of an "inferiority complex" is not found in conquering feelings of inferiority, but in learning how one has conquered oneself *already,* i.e., getting in touch with the energy of the *unacknowledged* brute inside who is making the rest of the person feel inferior. Actually, there are no "weaklings." Every so-called weakling is

50

already using enormous power, but unfortunately it is pointed in the wrong direction. The secret, therefore, is to discover the unacknowledged side of the existing polarity, not to give the person some "new" strength.

Failure to acknowledge both sides of every polarity often results in "projecting" one of them onto the external environment. How many people see the world as full of brutes who are all out to get them? Few realize in this connection how often they keep *themselves* from getting what they supposedly want. It is not just that the "world" refuses to cooperate. They may be refusing to cooperate with themselves. So even when they do get what they want, they seldom know what to do with it. Usually, however, they fail and then blame the world for it. "Idealism" is always having shipwrecks on rocks that it never realizes are of its own making.

Once both sides of a polarity are acknowledged, then it is possible to discover the empty space, the balancing point, between them. The secret of Zen is in learning to make this acknowledgement and then disappear into the empty space between the polarities. This is the second way of understanding the Here and Now, as the empty space between the poles of past and future. The goal is to discover that emptiness and learn to live in it, like a hole or cave in the center of yourself. Get in touch with this hole and work on enlarging it. You may not be a saddhu living in a cave in the Himalayas, but you can live just as well in the cave that is yourself.

51

As a Gestalt exercise, try reversing some of your polarities and see how it feels. Sort out some characteristic life patterns and for one day reverse them. Do exactly the opposite of what you usually do. You can do it only in your imagination, as you did in the earlier exercise of taking a walk through a forest, but it is better if you can actually do it. If you do, Saturdays or Sundays are usually best because of greater freedom to experiment. If you usually get up early, get up late. If you usually dress in "nice" clothes, dress in sloppy ones. If you usually fix breakfast for other people, let them fix their own. After a while you will get a feeling for the exercise. You may discover that you really enjoy doing the opposite of what you usually do. All kinds of unacknowledged poles may rise to the surface. Try them out and see what happens. With some of them it will become obvious that your behavior in the future could very well be somewhere between the poles rather than always on one side, which creates a terrible strain on the system.

Explore and own all your polarities, even those related to your search for Enlightenment. It is possible, for example, to "push yourself" too hard in the search for truth. Whenever you push, you push against your own resistances and all resistances are not bad. The part that is slowing you down may be at least as wise as the part that wants you to hurry up and "get there." The push and the pull bring each other into existence. Diminishing the one will necessarily diminish the other.

By the same token, any time when you want to "get rid" of something in yourself, a bad habit or whatever, try getting more acquainted with the thing that you want to get rid of in an appreciative as well as a resentful way.

Appreciation-resentment is a basic Gestalt polarity that is of use anywhere that a conflict occurs either internally or externally. Maybe the bad habit has at least something good about it that you will have to absorb in some way before you can get rid of it. Or perhaps you don't need to get rid of it at all. Self-mutilation is a futile activity. "If your eye offends you, pluck it out," should be replaced by: "If your eye offends you, try becoming your eye and talk back to the rest of you."

Dreams are particularly interesting in terms of such polarities. You are not only yourself and your friends in your dreams; you are your enemies, villains, and monsters as well. Your polar opposites are still you. As an exercise, try experiencing yourself as any person, power, or thing in your dreams that you find troublesome or objectionable. Experience what you like as well as what you don't like about the role. If it is a monster, feel the power. Sometimes the monster pursuing you in your dreams has something that you need and that is why it is chasing you. What you lack (power) is what the monster has.

As you consider the objectionable entity, whatever it is, appreciate it as well as resent it and realize that you are appreciating yourself. Better still, dramatize the dialogue. How does it feel to have the monster's power instead of being the victim of it? Act out possible conversations between such a part and yourself. Most of the problems in dreams come from blocked interactions. Establishing a relation between the parts removes the block. Dreams are homeostatic as well as enstatic. They are relational (Part II) as well as integral (Part I). So get in touch with your polarities, as revealed in your dreams. "To be or not to be" is *not* the question. Hamlet was a bit unbalanced.

53

A technique for reversing polarities in an interpersonal context is role reversal. This is especially effective in arguments. Each person plays the other person's role and tries to carry on the same kind of dialogue as before. This exercise can wake you up to how easy it is to *assume* that you know what the other person is saying. As in other polarity reversing exercises, the point is to set up a more honest dialogue between the two sides. Quarrels tend to take place between phantoms. They tend to be two one-sided conversations going on at the same time. The "other" side is not really acknowledged. You may discover just how convincing the other person's position really is. It certainly becomes easier to negotiate whatever contract is possible between you. The disagreement remaining at least becomes a more authentic one.

Such a role reversal exercise has the advantage of being a *self correcting* feedback process and is likely to be more beneficial than all kinds of external interference by moral guardians. The necessary corrective is usually found within the situation itself if real dialogue is established. Dialogue, even disagreement, is essential to the operation of every system. Every system entails "restraint" in that sense. That is one of the discoveries of cybernetics.

To suppose that a quarrel between two people is settled by the triumph of one or the other is similar to the religious illusion that self-mutilation works because it removes the "offending member." What usually happens is that the potentially valuable feedback disappears and the offending member only comes back in a more disguised form anyway. The dialogue then becomes a useless harangue directed at someone else who becomes a mere projection of the same old offending member. This is how churches get so

56

many "offending members." Triumph over sin is usually a shallow victory.

One of the exercises described by Castaneda is "listening to the holes between the sounds."[5] Don Juan gives Carlos a pipeful of psychedelic smoking mixture first, but you can begin instead with some general meditative exercises. Listening to the holes between sounds can be done anywhere, but it is probably easiest when you go for a walk somewhere in a park or in the country. If you can't find anywhere else, try a cemetery, which is often the quietest and most undisturbed place around. Be sure that you have plenty of time and are not rushed. Sit down and listen to the sounds around you. Listen carefully for a while and notice as many different sounds as possible and enjoy them. Listen to the world's music. Then switch from listening to the sounds to listening to the spaces *between* the sounds. A new world may open up for you. It becomes a different kind of hearing The silence makes its own kind of music. Listening to nothing at all can be enjoyable.

Don Juan facilitates listening to the "holes" by playing a special stringed instrument that he calls a "spirit catcher," but you can use a bell with similar effect. Listen to its sound as the silence between the sounds, or as the sound between the silences. It works both ways. It is as if a hole is created. See if you can get a feeling for these holes. Explore them as you would mysterious and fascinating caves. With some practice you can learn to do this anywhere. Even the clatter of dishes in the kitchen can open up another dimension. The universe is full of holes, and music is flowing out of every one of them. Don Juan also points out how shadows provide a visual equivalent, particularly when you overlap them by crossing your eyes and looking into the space between them. Shadows on a sunny day are a world of their own. In any of these holes, auditory or visual, you can learn what it means to be "Mr. In-Between."

In the following exercise you don't need to do anything. It is an exercise about nothing at all. Simply notice your breathing without changing it in any way. Just follow yourself along, watching everything but without interfering. Take it in, but don't try to figure anything out and don't try to do anything differently. There is no one whose approval you need by doing the exercise properly. Just open your awareness to what is already going on.

Soon you will experience difficulty staying with the exercise. Your attention will wander. You will begin thinking about other things. Don't try to keep it from wandering. Let it go, but also try to watch it wandering, too. Notice particularly the spaces between the thoughts. Attune yourself to these empty spaces and enjoy them while they are there without trying to keep them there. As you progress in this exercise, you will notice that these empty spaces grow larger and larger. Try to hollow out a (non)place for your (un)self. You are the You_niverse.

DOING THE YO_U_NIVERSE

You are a simultaneous happening of a myriad of events, constantly overlapping with each other. You are an evermoving coordination of interdependent parts, interdepending in turn with the environment around you. Without interchange with your environment you die in only a few seconds. "It all depends." The balance shifts continually and in many instances automatically as internal and external changes take place. No action that you undertake is simply an action. It is a reaction, a responding, an adjustment in the direction of equilibrium.

Walter B. Cannon coined the word "homeostasis" in 1932 in his book *The Wisdom of the Body* where he makes a distinction between equilibrium and homeostasis. The former, he says, refers to a fairly exact meaning applied to simple physico-chemical states, in closed systems where known forces are balanced. The latter refers to the "relatively constant" condition of complex organisms involving the cooperative working of parts together.[6] Psychologically as well as physically, you are such a homeostatic system. As the French phenomenologist Merleau-Ponty says: "Whether a system of motor or perceptual powers, our body is not an object for an 'I think,' it is a grouping of lived through meanings which moves toward its equilibrium."[7]

To become aware of your own interdependence, stand in what for you is a normal standing position. Become aware of your body. Begin to walk around. Now slow yourself down as if you are in a slow-motion movie that is getting slower and slower until you are hardly moving at all. You will begin to notice various balancing activities of which you are not normally aware. Notice how you waver (oscillate) constantly forward and backward, right and left, with different parts of your body. Notice the way in which virtually every part of you is put to use in this balancing act. Even shutting your eyes has a sizable effect on how well you are able to maintain your balance.

Now stop walking and stand as still as possible. Notice how you are still balancing. Notice how tightening different parts of your body affects your balance. If you are hunching your back, your knees tend to lock. Affecting one part of the system also affects other parts far distant from it. You are a miniature ecological system. The interdependent functioning of the parts spreads any effects over the whole. Get some feeling for how you interfere most with the smooth functioning of the balancing process. You may contract your chest in order to protect yourself (understandably) from parental or other authoritative demands (including the one to stand up straight), but you may not be aware of what this contraction is doing *against* you, namely, shutting off your air supply and putting a strain on your balancing process and the speed with which you are able to adjust to any threat from the outside. Remember what was said earlier about the body as a picture of your mind. Your mind, like your body, is a balancing act that sometimes interferes with itself, and the interferences tend to show up in the same places time after time. They become your character traits, and character in this sense leads, ironically, to instability. Without the free and instant communication of all of your parts with each other, you become a pushover.

The *I Ching,* an ancient book of Chinese wisdom, is also known as *The Book of Changes.* The seeker after wisdom consults the book in terms of various possible pairs of "trigrams," or trios of solid or broken lines. There are eight basic trigrams, which make for sixty-four possible pairs. Any advice given by the *I Ching* is the result of the interaction of this pair of trigrams. Thus the *I Ching* can properly be called not only *The Book of Changes* but *The Book of Interchanges.*

There is no end to the applications of the model of interchange. Not only are you a system of interchanges within yourself and between you and the physical environment around you, but you also function as an interchanging part of social systems as well. Without other people in fact, you would have no meaning. Not only do you depend on others for physical services; you also depend on them for your very definition of what it means to be human, for speech itself, for the very way in which life makes sense to you. Interchange with your social environment is as inevitable as interchange with your physical environment. The space between people (the field for interchange) is the most important thing that they have in common.

Every human experience is an interchange of some sort. There is no action without a reaction. There is good reason to be suspicious of any ethical system that is "one-sided," that is not built on the foundation of interchange. "Generosity," for example, often has an expensive price tag, as the history of the Christian Church demonstrates. Generosity often means that the people doing the supposed *giving* are blind to what they are *getting.* The only way to support someone who is leaning on you is to lean back. So who is depending on whom? *Every* action is an interaction.

Both individual and social organisms continually oscillate back and forth between polarities and complexes of polarities in the maintenance of balance or homeostasis. Freedom is not, as some leaders of the human potential movement would have you think, a mere matter of getting rid of inhibitions, which can do more damage than good by unloosing energies that neither the individual nor the group is ready to absorb or utilize. Freedom is a function of balance and of the ease with which that balance takes place.

To experience that kind of freedom, return to the mantram described earlier. Remember the three parts of the OM sound (ah-oh-oom). This time focus on the "oh" sound. Notice the way in which that sound has moved forward to the front of your mouth and seems to make a cave there. Notice that it is neither inside nor outside, that it has openings in both directions. In this sense the OM mantram may be considered as the balancing point of the You*niverse*, that sound that is between all sounds, the wordless word. Again, it makes no difference what it means. It means Nothing just as easily as it meant the All in the earlier exercise. It is the space between. It is the emptiness.

Something similar can be experienced with OM MANI PADME HUM, which can be translated as "Jewel of the Lotus," but also, according to some Tantric sources, as male and female sexual organs. It is the meeting of opposites. See if you can experience it as the sound between the sounds, the homeostatic sound, the sound of the You*niverse.

One of the distinctive features of Gestalt therapy is its operational confidence that the organism will take care of itself as long as it stays with present experience. An unfinished situation has a way of returning untii it is attended to. It cannot be escaped. It is as if the organism has a built in, largely unconscious sense of imbalance and of what it takes to "correct" itself and refuses to go on to anything else until this correction is made.

Everyone has remarkable and persistent self-regulating powers. It is not necessary to have well-defined, external moral standards. The needed action is always in the process of emerging alongside the problem. The organism attends to its own lacks almost automatically. Furthermore, when a potential solution appears, the best test of whether it is *the* solution or not is in how it feels and how it works. It is similar to the way in which you automatically try to correct yourself when you stumble. When everything is operating homeostatically, an action feels right when you do it, but when something is out of kelter, you automatically notice it and try to do something about it. And you keep doing something about it until you know that the balance is restored, even if that means picking yourself back up again. The sense of balance is as much a psychological and social function as it is a physical one.

All one needs to do is the "Here and Now I am aware . . ." exercise described earlier in order to see how this works. If you do the exercise for more than a few minutes, the chaos of disconnected thoughts tends to fade out in favor of something more organized. It may be quite persistent. Once you begin thinking about it, it will not go away. It could be anything from feeling an itch that you cannot ignore to a feeling of dissatisfaction about a relationship in which you are involved. The point is that all you need to do is to pay attention to such unfinished situations, to maintain your present awareness, instead of ignoring it or trying to force it out of the way because it is unpleasant. In either of those cases "it" will soon be back anyway, begging again for attention. Very big problems will require attention over a considerable period of time, but just as an itch will disappear when you give attention to it, so will other problems. All you have to do is to get in touch with the homeostatic mechanisms that are already inside you. The signal system is already there.

Something of the same sort works on a social level. Homeostasis gives a new meaning to ethics as well as to psychology generally. As suggested earlier, ethics becomes a matter of response, of interchange, not a one-sided ethics of ideals and principles. To carry this a step further, ethics as response means sensitivity to socially unfinished situations. The by-line of the *Rolling Stone* newspaper reads: "All the news that fits," rather than the usual: "All the news that's fit." The fitting action is the action that corrects the balance. Here, too, if an action fits, it feels right and the matter is finished. You can go on to something else. If it does not fit, it feels wrong and the matter becomes a nagging social problem. It does not go away. It will be back until it is finished or until it destroys the equilibrium of the system. It will be the same old moral dilemma time after time. That is how feedback as a self-regulating process works, whether individual or social. Ethics always has a homeostatic as well as an enstatic quality. The You*niversal virtue is responsibility, with an emphasis on the responding.

ENJOYING THE YO*U*NIVERSE

Not only is the world full of sacred objects; it is also full of sacred "non-objects." Polarities not only inter*act*, they inter*play*, which is the source of the beauty of the Yo*u*niverse. The Yo*u*niverse is a dance in the space *between* the things that are "there."

One of the greatest resources in facilitating the enjoyment of emptiness is Zen. Zen is different from the techniques described under the first Youniversal. While the end result may not be all that different, there is a definite difference in language and method. Zen realizes that emptiness is spread all through the dualities of the world of the 10,000 forms. And Zen is especially aware of the dangers of tipping consciousness to one side or the other and losing one's balance in the process.

Achieving Satori in Zen is not so much a moving into or beyond the world as it is a dwelling *between* it. "The famous Tokusan was sitting outside his Master's house on the verandah, striving to accomplish Zen. His Master asked from within, 'Why don't you come in?' 'It is dark,' said Tokusan. A candle was lighted and handed to him, but as he was about to take it, the Master blew it out. Tokusan was enlightened."[8] So it is neither the question nor the answer as such that counts but what happens between them. For Zen that is the place of joy.

68

Consider the following Zen Koans (instructive stories).
Do not be content with an intellectual understanding. Get
a feeling for the space that they open up in the interaction
between the parties of the dialogue.

One day as Manjusri stood outside the gate, the
Buddha called to him, "Manjusri, why do you not enter?"
Manjusri replied, "I do not see myself outside. Why
enter?"[9]

One day a young novice said to Patriarch Hogen,
"My name is Echo, and I would like to ask Your Reverence
what is meant by the name Buddha?" Hogan merely said,
"Oh, so you are Echo are you?"[10]

A simple exercise that will introduce you to the world between things as a place where you can play is to hum, sing, or whistle deliberately off key. You can do it while engaged in other activities, too. You can do it as you walk to school or work or as you do the laundry or take a bath. It is especially useful when you are frustrated, depressed, or bored, and is a good remedy for "thinking too much." Play in the cracks between the keys instead of on the keys themselves. Make up your own tunes. Try consciously to invent a tune that is as ugly as possible. Be as unmusical as you possibly can. Squeak, grunt, groan, gobble, or fart. Try to make it the worst song ever composed. Set up small ensembles if you like and do chamber unmusic. You may discover that "ugly is beautiful." You may discover some of the humor and creativity of playing in some of those in-between places.

Within you are many yous, each struggling perhaps for superiority. If so, it is one more futile struggle, like the one between the supposed angel on one shoulder and the devil on the other. They call each other into existence even in the act of stamping each other out. However, there is another possibility, i.e., in the space between them rather than in themselves. The unity of the self is not in the triumph of the "will" or any of the many selves but in allowing the selves like so many roles played on a stage each to have a part without getting lost in that particular part by identifying exclusively with it. That is one lesson in Herman Hesse's novel *Steppenwolf*. Harry Haller, the protagonist, has to learn not to choose between the roles of wolf and man so much as to acknowledge both and to learn to live between them.

As an exercise that you can do over an extended period of time, try to become aware of all the roles that you yourself play in life and then stand in the space between those roles and watch them "do their thing." As you go about your daily affairs, notice when any one of them is making an appearance. Stay in the silence of the audience and watch what happens onstage. Don't try to rewrite the script. It is possible and may even be inevitable that you may live on many different levels at once. It is a waste of your time and energy when you try to identify with only one of your cast of characters and eliminate all the rest.

Consider instead the possibility that each role rises to the surface of consciousness at the precise moment when at least something from that role is *needed*. Every time a new role appears onstage, ask what has been missing and what this new player provides. Perhaps your multidimensionality can be (homeostatically) enjoyed. There is certainly something comic as well as futile about the way in which each of your yous engages in combat with the others. So don't take your selves too seriously; learn to smile at them. See how much you can open up the empty space between the roles. As with Harry Haller, perhaps you need to sit back and enjoy the Magic Theater that you are.

Not only are the rituals of a society the holographic means of bringing the society together; they are the homeostatic means of maintaining delicate balances. A ritual carefully tips the balances one way or another in order to establish an equilibrium that is missing or at least jeopardized. The shaman is one who specializes not only in uniting the tribe under the sacred symbols but in maintaining the balances between the tribe and the powers of nature. Everything animate or inanimate has energy of its own to be contended with in preserving the balance. One must be especially careful not to disturb the balances overmuch. Spiritual activities, too, are exchanges. For every favor a price must be paid. What emerges, therefore, is the same kind of moving, spontaneous equilibrium already mentioned in which the ultimate test of the ritual is in what unfinished business remains afterward. When the ritual is effective, it feels right and the harmony is re-established. When it is not, it is obvious and further action is called for.

A good model for understanding rituals and the homeostatic arts in general is the dance. Dance is a moving equilibrium. It is never located, never fixed. It is not so much a series of steps or positions as it is what happens in the spaces between the steps. Failed rituals and clumsiness are the same thing, a locking in place that results in lost balance. Dance is always done with grace, without strain, between here and there, thinking and feeling, time and space. Even in martial arts like Aikedo and Tai Chi, what began as a battle ends in grace and dance. It is in dance more than anywhere else that freedom as homeostasis becomes clear. The image of perfect freedom is not the rebel but the dancer, as in the dance of the Hindu God,

Shiva. A rebel is always condemned to the "other" side of the polarity. A dancer moves freely and unencumbered into the emptiness of the Youniverse, balancing between the polarities. The most basic of all tribal rituals are those that in one way or another involve dancing.

Find a place where you can have privacy and a phonograph and put on some music that you find relaxing. With practice you can do the exercise to wilder and faster music, but initially it is better to use something quieter. Be sure to wear comfortable, non-restricting clothing if you wear any at all so that you can pay attention to the natural movement of your body.

First, sit or lie down and listen to the music for a while. Listen, as in the earlier exercise, to the spaces between the sounds as well as to the sounds themselves. Then, when you feel ready, allow yourself to begin to move with the music. As you move, notice the space between you and the environment. This is the realm of dance, this evermoving, always balancing space. Do not try consciously to do anything. Allow yourself to be moved *by* the music and your surroundings as much as to move toward them. Try to discover the harmony, the moving balance, between you and your surroundings. Also, discover the balance between movement and stillness. Don't push and don't hold back. Experiment with all the polarities that you can find, oscillating back and forth between them until you can find your space. Allow the polarities to speak to each other through you. Let them interact and be their point of meeting. Open up that "space between" and move into it. Feel its edges. Feel its freedom.

You can also dance this way with someone else if you feel comfortable doing so. That provides another dimension, the space between you (plural). Move toward or away from the other person as it feels comfortable. Let the space between you speak. This is already, of course, the genius of much of the dancing in the world of rock music. You do not have to touch each other in order to be together. You can share the space. When you do this with several people at the same time, you have the beginning of a ritual.

The physical immobility of audiences in concert halls is sad to see. It is, of course, understandable that audiences should be relatively quiet or no one could hear the music, but that is no reason for remaining immobile. Anyone disturbed by other members of the audience moving or dancing to the music might be better off listening to it at home on the radio or stereo. Someone may someday stage a performance of "classical" music in which the audience is free to dance. Many people dance secretly while listening to it at home. Why not in the concert hall?

It is unfortunate that Christianity never gave a significant place to dance. Can you imagine a bishop dancing? The shaman, on the other hand, is not a shaman unless he dances. Dance is interplay. As such it is the homeostatic act *par excellence*. Whenever you dance, you participate in the You̲niverse.

PART III
THE THIRD YOUNIVERSAL:

The Youniverse is ecstatic.
You move and grow beyond yourself into the
Youniverse.
The Youniverse is the You_niverse_.

The Youniverse is organic, continually moving and growing. It is a process that never stands still. The emphasis here is not so much on unity (Part I) or interdependence (Part II) as it is on energy flow or current. The Youniverse is "negentropic," always beyond redundancy, useless repetition and decay. The Youniverse is not only found *in* (Part I) and *between* (Part II), but *beyond*. The Youniverse is the You*niverse*. It is an *open* rather than *closed* system. It transports you beyond yourself into a strange and marvelous world that cannot finally be anticipated. It is surprise and excitement. The You*niverse* is ecstatic.

You are not an "object" so much as a "flowing beyond." You never stand still long enough for you to get a good still-shot of yourself. You are not quite the same person today that you were yesterday. You are always moving, continually making and remaking yourself. What made sense to you yesterday may not make sense to you now. What makes sense to you now may not make sense to you tomorrow. In Gestalt terms this is a never ending process of "configuring," forming and reforming the world into coherent shapes or patterns (*Gestalten*). A gestalt takes shape in one moment only to be modified in the next in a continual process of growth and development. Neurosis is inability to complete an "old" gestalt so that you can go on to a new one.

Putting the same thing in terms of communication theory, everything intelligible decays constantly from useful information and patterns into meaningless disorder and chaos. This is called *entropy*, the tendency of any system to degrade toward inert uniformity. Consciousness as system is either closed or open, depending on whether it is able to make new sense out of the chaos, whether it can adjust to new situations. An open system is organic; it is related to what is beyond it. In terms of energy, the amount of energy generated in an open system can exceed the amount of energy lost. In an open system the energy can be exchanged and thereby renewed. This is what is called *negentropy*.

This is as much a cultural phenomenon as it is a physical and psychological one. A work of art lives only so long as it is "beyond" its explanations. If it can be exhaustively analyzed, described, or performed, it can be declared dead and finished. Shakespeare's plays will live only so long as they elude any final interpretation. Art is always beyond itself, as is every other really conscious act. As a Zen master once told the ecological theorist Gregory Bateson: "To become accustomed to anything is a terrible thing."[1]

On one level this is what communication theory and, more broadly, systems thinking is all about. So far as that is concerned, on one level systems thinking is what this book is all about. The first Youniversal concerns the definition of a whole, a system. The second concerns the multiple input quality of a system, the source of feedback. And the third concerns energy flow and the ability of an open system to "survive," to transcend itself. As long as a person is alive (surviving), (s)he is in some way an open system, continually opening to the environment.

Survival *is* opening to what is around you, from the air that you breathe to the information that you receive. Survival is opening to what is on the other side of you. Survival is not just balance, a "steady state," but a *moving* balance. Survival is change. The old self is constantly destroyed, and the new self is constantly created. The You*niverse* is always full of such movement.

From earliest times man has struggled to depict movement in the cosmos. This is evident in petroglyphs. Spirals, animal tracks, and mazes all require a certain amount of movement on the part of the viewer in order to comprehend their mysteries. They are not, in any event, stationary models. Movement is an inescapable part of them.

The modern Irish poet William Butler Yeats found the movement of history and the cosmos in the gyre, a cone shaped spiral that widens constantly from its apex to its outer limit. For Yeats this limit is the place where the wheeling falcon reaches such a height and distance that he can no longer hear the voice of the falconer who released him. Meaning is lost and a new one is called for. Yeats saw history as a double gyre kind of chain, one gyre widening from apex to outer limit while another gyre, laid over it, is doing the opposite, narrowing to its apex, and so on in an endless opening and closing chain. More recently scientists have used still other spiral forms, helixes and double helixes, as models for basic life processes.

In the first Youniversal time is eternity. In the second it is the specious present between past and future. In the third it is the ever flowing river. Everything is always new and changing, whether it is you, history, or the cosmos. This section therefore deals with movement ("motility"), with energy, with excitement. The You_universe_ is ecstatic.

KNOWING THE YO*UNIVERSE*

Outside the door, the universe is waiting to have a word with you. "Be sensitive to everything sensible. Absorb everything that you can," says a voice from a dream. And yet it is difficult to open the door. Some people open it only a crack. Others do not open it at all, preferring instead to stay in the room and talk to themselves.

Internal dialogue is sometimes helpful and necessary, but it can also be detrimental, especially when it turns to attacking oneself. While you are scolding or judging yourself, you become a courtroom, the doors of which are locked. No one can get in and you can't get out. And judges, at least of this sort, dislike backtalk (feedback), either from anyone inside or outside the court. Thus the internal dialogue becomes a frustrating monologue with the judge doing all the talking and the defendant listening, perhaps trying to make excuses, but mostly just feeling tired, awkward, and guilty. It is a closed system and energy is lost.

The judge is usually a "retroflected" parent, teacher, priest, or some combination of them, someone who silenced you as a child and who still silences you even though the silencer may no longer be present in the flesh. When you saw that person's eyes on you, you stopped what you were doing. Your awareness of your surroundings disappeared; you were only aware of yourself and what was wrong with you. You were cast out of the Garden. And since that voice inside you came originally from outside and is not really in that sense your own, since it was what someone else thought of you and not what you yourself thought, you naturally spend a lot of time and energy making lame excuses and trying to evade the sentence. But the attempt to justify yourself is futile, and you never consider the possibility that it may be the judge who is really at fault.

It is far better to admit the world than to admit your "offenses." This requires an understanding of *admission as "letting in" rather than "confessing."* Admitting is opening the door and letting the outside in, or letting yourself go outside, as the case may be. This kind of admitting also has its problems, because what is on the other side of the door is sometimes painful, but it is usually better to run the risk of being hurt in the world than continually to hurt and torture yourself. Or to put it another way, it is usually better to learn what to do or not to do from the world and your experience in it than to try to learn from that demanding voice that will never be satisfied with what you do anyway. This is the difference between feedback and retroflection. Despite superficial similarities, they are not the same thing at all. Feedback consists of various signals, whether negative or positive, that enhance your ability to react and to grow. Retroflection is a struggle against oneself that *prevents* action and growth. Feedback makes for survival, for an increase of energy. Retroflection makes for guilt and deadness, for loss of energy. Retroflection is a closed system. Why is it that the gates of paradise are always depicted as being locked? And why is it that it is always someone else who decides whether you get in?

An exercise that may help to get in touch with the process of "admission" is to go for a special kind of walk. Find a place that you would like to explore, one where you can be alone. The rule is that you move around and explore your environment *only* so long as your attention is with the environment. If you notice that you are no longer paying attention to the environment but are thinking about something else, a problem that may be troubling you or whatever, just sit down, shut your eyes, and go on thinking about it. Then when you notice that your attention is going back to the environment, that your curiosity about something external is returning, open your eyes, get up, and start moving around again. Keep the exercise going for as long as you like.

Nothing is wrong with thinking as such, and this exercise may give you the time and occasion to think something out to its conclusion instead of stopping half way through, which is the customary practice for many people. But when you are too busy with your thoughts, you become too wrapped up in yourself, and you tend to see the world, if at all, as a mere reflection of the thoughts that you had already about it and not as something new and marvelous. This exercise helps to focus on the new and marvelous.

Do you notice while doing this exercise that it is getting late and that you really should be getting back home, or that you should be getting more out of the exercise, or that you really should do this exercise more often? Retroflection is usually at work whenever you hear yourself saying: "I should . . ." Does the voice sound like that of anyone you know (or knew)? Whose voice is it? Try talking back to that voice and see what happens.

89

To put it more positively, explore the difference between retroflecting and giving yourself permission or "allowing." Allowing does not necessarily mean "becoming uninhibited," but it does mean opening out and touching. In Gestalt terms, the first Youniversal concerns "confluence," becoming one, coinciding with your surroundings. The third Youniversal concerns "contact," opening your experience to what is there. The point is to admit, to let in. The point is to allow.

When you admit the world, when you allow yourself to be who you are and do what you do with your eyes wide open, the world will always speak to you. Someone once had a dream in which he climbed for what seemed to be forever up the sheer face of a cliff until he finally reached a ledge. As he looked over it, he saw a small boy standing there who said, "Let me help you," to which he replied, "No, thanks. I can do it myself. I've climbed all this way already, and all that I have to do is to pull myself up on the ledge." The boy insisted, "No, you don't understand. Let me help you." Again he rejected the offer, but as he started to throw his leg over the edge, it crumbled and he fell.

The following is a Sufi story:

Nasrudin, ferrying a pedant across a piece of rough water, said something ungrammatical to him. "Have you ever studied grammar?" asked the scholar.
"No."
"Then half of your life has been wasted."
A few minutes later Nasrudin turned to the passenger. "Have you ever learned to swim?"
"No. Why?"
"Then *all* of your life is wasted—we are sinking."[2]

One of the easiest ways to lose contact with the environment is to get lost in "explanations" to the point where explanations become more real than the experience that is being explained. Explanations are like most lectures; they tend to be empty, dead, totally lacking in energy. Meaning does not stand *behind* experience as some kind of presupposition of it, as it does for the pedant in the story, as if first you learn all the lessons and then you "apply" them to the world. It is not nearly so important whether you know *why* you are doing something so long as you know *how* to do it. And in order to know *how* to do something, it is necessary to open up your experience. As Rumi, the Sufi mystic, put it: "He who tastes not, knows not."

Retroflection is as much a problem for the body as for the mind. The door to the outside can be shut in many ways: by squinting your eyes, tightening your mouth or neck, by tensing your shoulders or your anus or genitals. Notice whether you are doing any of these things right now. If you are, try to become aware of how you are doing it by exaggerating the tightness and then relaxing it. Notice what kind of feelings arise when you do this.

Focus especially on your breathing. Perls defines anxiety as "the experience of breathing difficulty during any blocked excitement. It is the experience of trying to get more air into lungs immobilized by muscular constrictions of the thoracic cage."[3] Because of the way that "self-control" causes most breathing problems in the first place, the best breathing exercises are those that interfere least with natural processes. Again, focus on your breathing without trying to change anything. Simply be aware. Or notice a particular part of your breathing apparatus, without trying to change anything. As thoughts or feelings rise to the surface, just let them go. Try releasing them with your breath as well as your mind. Express them in sounds or words if you like and watch them fade away into the distance. Even visualize them. Imagine that you are opening a door and letting them out. Let them all out with the release of your breath. Don't hold any of them back. As in meditation, the secret is not in learning to stop your thoughts but in learning to let go of them. Trying to stop them only keeps them from leaving. Open the door and they will all eventually leave of their own accord.

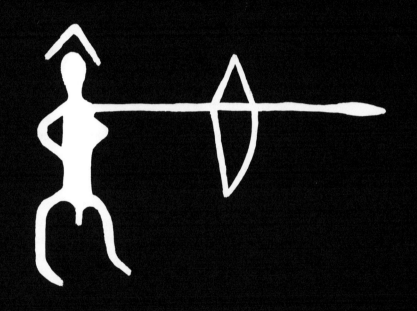

Where judging ends, humor begins. Humor begins with not taking yourself so seriously and thereby opening yourself to the Yo_universe_. Is it any accident that the industrial monarchs of the nineteenth and early twentieth centuries were grim, tight-lipped people? They seldom laughed and never learned to play. They lost touch with their environment and were therefore blind to their own creations; exploitation, pollution, and ecological disaster. How strange that those who feared "filth" so much were the creators of it on a scale never before known.

Engage in a Gestalt remembering exercise. Pick an experience that you find "unfinished" in some way and remember it in as great detail as you can, but as if it is happening now. Remember the setting as well as you can. Notice even minute details, everything that you can remember of what you saw, heard, and felt as well as what you thought. Open your memory. Remember how you felt when you said what you said. In this way relive the event from beginning to end but this time with your eyes wide open. As Perls puts it: "Repeating an action to the point of mastery is the essence of development."[4] Events that are painful may require many repeats before all the pain is gone, but seldom will you replay such an event without making some connection that will assist you in disposing of the unfinished business attached to it.

For Yeats' ancient Chinamen in his poem "Lapis Lazuli," who sit on the mountain witnessing the procession of history passing before them, even its tragic qualities become a comedy:

> There, on the mountain and the sky,
> On all the tragic scene they stare.

94

One asks for mournful melodies;
Accomplished fingers begin to play.
Their eyes mid many wrinkles, their eyes,
Their ancient, glittering eyes, are gay.[5]

Admission leads to humor. As Yeats describes it, even pain and tragedy become something other than that in the process of allowing them and becoming aware of them. In acknowledging, in accepting them, beauty and excitement open on the other side of them. In Gestalt therapy this is called finishing your unfinished situations; in the East it is called burning your Karma. In either case, the result of opening and allowing is joy, the state of bliss. The You*niverse* is ecstatic.

DOING THE YO*UNIVERSE*

Flexibility is an essential ingredient in the maintenance of an open system. Flexibility is the capacity for change. This has become the condition for human survival in the present age. Rigidity means death; flexibility means life. Rigidity is forcing the world or yourself to stay put in a strained position. It is refusal to change, to alter the "bias" of the system. Flexibility is softening and opening for survival. As stated in the *Tao te Ching*:

> A man is born gentle and weak.
> At death he is hard and stiff.
> Green plants are tender and filled with sap.
> At their death they are withered and dry.
> Therefore the stiff and unbending is the disciple of death.
> The gentle and yielding is the disciple of life.
> Thus an army without flexibility never wins a battle.
> A tree that is unbending is easily broken.
> The hard and strong will fall.
> The soft and weak will overcome.[6]

Judo does in fact make yielding, giving up, going with the flow, the way to gain victory. Many have noticed how, even in the Western world, the strong willed and determined "he-man" has given way to the softer, more pliable "she-man." It is an inevitable transformation given the demands of the present world. It was the he-man who created many of the world's ecological disasters. The secret is not in strength but in sensitivity, not in will power but in feeling.

As an exercise, try softening your contact with the world by focusing more on your feelings. The exercise can be done anytime and anywhere. You don't need to change what you are doing. Just focus on feelings instead of thoughts. Begin all your sentences with: "Here and Now I feel . . ." and fill in the blank with how you *feel*. Allow some space between the statements. Start another one only when you notice some change, even if it is a small one, in the feeling. Also notice how you lose contact with feelings when you launch into lengthy descriptions of *why* you feel that way. Or when you say: "Here and Now I feel *that* . . ." and then fill in the blank with a belief or thought instead of a feeling. Or when you put a "because" at the end of the statement and then give more explanations. Notice your feelings and how those feelings change as you notice them. Feelings change just as much as thoughts do.

Do this exercise when you feel distressed. Those feelings, too, will change as you notice them. The best way to "get out of a rut" is to open to it, to pay more attention to it rather than to try to ignore it or escape it. Be sure, however, to do the exercise long enough to get some results. If the feeling is a deep and unpleasant one, you may have to do it on the installment plan, but try to stay with your feelings until you do notice a change. It makes a difference when you soften your contact, when you allow your feelings to have full play. Too many people sit on their feelings with their thoughts. Learning is not thinking, as such; it is changing. And changing involves feeling your way.

The maintenance of flexibility has a great deal to do with the flow of energy and learning to go with that flow. Struggling against your own current will only exhaust you, so that you will have no energy left when you need it. To be able to stay with the evermoving Here and Now, you must "play it loose," neither faltering nor rushing, neither holding back nor leaping ahead too quickly.

The biggest single reason for either faltering or rushing is pain. The most difficult experiences to relive in the remembering exercise are those in which pain plays a prominent part. When the pain is too great to be experienced and accepted at the moment, it is carefully walled off from the rest of the self. While this removes the pain from direct awareness and may make the situation tolerable momentarily, it does not remove it from the system. Pain rises again and again to the surface only to be pushed back down again, and so it remains, locked in place and yet never really manageable. Ironically, fear of experiencing pain is exactly what is keeping it there. The child cannot let go of the teat even when it is dry, because that means being alone, so (s)he hangs on (understandably) exactly as hard as (s)he pushes away (understandably). (S)he is afraid to let go. (S)he cannot open the clenched mouth. And a clenched mouth cannot get what it now needs.

For some the fear of pain results in more faltering than rushing. They flinch at the present, because living in the present requires fully experiencing and letting go of the past, and that they cannot do. They hide in a useless past, refusing to come out, pretending to themselves that it is safer where they are. Life becomes a compulsive repetition of an event that is never completed. They become rigid and inflexible, frozen in their fear, ready to burst at any moment and using all their energy to prevent that happening. They alternate between frenzy and despair.

For others fear of pain leads mostly to rushing ahead impulsively, always mapping and planning for a future (either good or bad) that never quite arrives. They become so busy trying to get somewhere, so busy anticipating what they are going to do, that they never do anything. Some hope and others dread. For those who hope, when one goal is reached, it is immediately replaced by another and they never enjoy the present. Happiness is always somewhere ahead of them. For those who dread, like the child in the dentist's chair, they try to "hurry and get it over with," pushing desperately into the future in an effort to escape the pain, but the pain remains in the form of a feeling of impending doom (the next trip to the dentist).

In either case reality is always just around the corner, but the beautiful ideal or the terrible catastrophe moves away from them at exactly the rate that they rush madly toward it. They never reach the goal. Life is a drag. Then one day they realize that it now *is* the future. In a macabre way they have gotten their wish. Life has been such a rush that it is now nearly over, and the disillusionment of old age sets in. The time of life that could be the most beautiful becomes a terrible punishment.

The alternative is to go with the flow of the current, neither pushing nor pulling on it. This requires the flexibility to allow yourself to live your experiences fully, including those that are painful. The only way to win is to surrender. There is no way to get anywhere faster than your own current will carry you there.

Return once more to the basic awareness exercise. Again begin sentences with "Here and Now I am aware . . ." or perhaps simply "I am aware . . ." if you prefer. Notice particularly when you are leaving the present for either a past or a future that is removed from it. Do not try to keep yourself from going into the past, but do begin to get in touch with what in the past needs to be relived and experienced. If you are leaving the present for a future, notice what you may be avoiding in the present as you do this. *To the extent that you feel ready to do so*, notice your feelings as they arise, including any pains or constrictions that you may experience. When you allow these feelings to come to the surface and express them, your experience moves toward completion.

You may experience the release of a great deal of locked-in energy as you engage in this exercise. Perls describes such experiences in terms of what he calls the "layers of the neurosis."[7] The last two of these layers in progressing toward cure are first the "implosive" or death layer and finally the "explosive" or life layer. In the implosive layer one gets beyond the "impasse" that characterizes earlier efforts to deal with the problem. The implosion is a caving in, a collapsing, a time of anguish, pain, and the fear of death. If the unfinished situation is one that involves an unbearable amount of pain, professional help or at least that of friends may be necessary. It is certainly not the purpose of this book to replace the need for qualified professionals. It is essential, in any case, to have a supporting and nourishing environment. It is also essential not to push yourself beyond what you are ready for.

The implosion itself does not mean, however, that

100

anything has gone wrong. It is very different from the self-destructive collapse that is brought about by pushing oneself beyond what one is ready for. Perls points out that once one comes into contact with the implosive layer, a strange thing happens almost automatically. The implosion becomes an explosion. Death becomes life. In terms of this section of the book, the energy that has been working against you finally comes to a dead end and reverses itself. It becomes your own again. It may be an explosion into grief, anger, orgasm, or joy and laughter depending on the kind of constriction being released. It is in these explosions according to Perls that the authentic personality emerges. The world becomes alive and exciting. It is in these moments that you go beyond yourself. The Y*ouniverse* becomes ecstatic.

To speak of the world as alive and exciting may sound incongruous with the goals of the religions of the East, which sometimes make it sound as if the Youniversal trip is no great fun. In Buddhism, for example, desire is described as a trap. The only way to eliminate suffering is to eliminate desire, and so forth. "Desire," however, should not be confused with "feeling." They are completely different entities, as different as rape is from making love. When Eastern religions speak of eliminating desire, they are not speaking of eliminating "feelings," at least as described in this book. Feeling is a surrender to what is beyond oneself. Desire is "attachment," a grabbing and hanging on to what does not really exist at all, a phantom, a projection. Attachments in this sense are exactly what interfere with real feeling. Feeling is an opening to the present. Desire is a closing off of that awareness, a constriction of it.

Those who have freed themselves from desire in this sense are not those who have hardened themselves and closed themselves off to what is around them but those who have softened themselves, made themselves more pliable and receptive to what is around them, who are capable of feeling more, not less, than others. Those who are really free from desire are those who can move, who can dance. Flexibility is motility; the ability to change is the ability to move. The one who feels is the one who neither pushes nor pulls either on the self or the world. Moving with the current is an enjoyable trip.

It is important to remember that you cannot *make* yourself flexible. All that you can *make* is clumsiness and awkwardness. Flexibility is allowed, not forced. All you have to do is to sit back and let it happen or, to be more exact, let *you* happen. As a good exercise in this respect, notice the maze on the preceding page. However, instead of rushing in and "solving" it as quickly as possible, begin at the entrance and let it *lead* you in. There is no need to force your way to the center like Cortez "exploring" Mexico. Nor is there any need to try to figure it out ahead of time. The trip itself is enjoyable. This exercise is for the purpose of maximizing softness and flexibility, not expectations and goal orientation.

Do this exercise any time when you notice that you are "pushing yourself" too hard. Even in terms of your expressed goals, you are likely to get there faster by being softer and more flexible than by "driving" yourself. Certainly you will enjoy it more when you do get there. If you are doing a meditation exercise and get frustrated because you cannot "silence" the internal voice, consider how you would "silence" a child who is crying in the night, not by yelling and trying to *force* the child to be quiet, but by being soft and soothing. Even visualize yourself soothing and caressing that child until (s)he goes to sleep and all is still.

Ecstasy is allowed, not coerced. It comes only by softening, by opening, by becoming more flexible. It comes to those who learn to bend with the breeze. It comes to those who learn to go with the flow of their own current. Flexibility is the Y<u>ouniversal</u> virtue.

ENJOYING THE YO*UNIVERSE*

The Yo*universe* is ecstatic. Ek-stasis to the Greeks referred to the flight of the soul from the body, the flight from the world of particulars to the world of universals. Ecstasy is the act of going beyond one's ordinary self. Ecstasy is nonordinary reality. Everything is contrary to expectation. It is the paradigm of energy itself, always beyond itself. An open system, a moving balance, is always open to the new and different.

Shamanism has developed ecstasy into a distinctive religious tradition.[8] The multifarious activities of the shaman, from healing to art, are joined by his mystical trips to the other world, i.e., the place where he is beyond himself. He goes there in order to bring back power and information that is useful to him and to others, especially the sick. He goes there because he finds it enjoyable.

The passageway to this world is sometimes described as a hole in the sky through which a kind of "world axis" passes. This hole bears resemblances to the "black holes" described by astronomers in that anything that comes close to it is drawn irresistibly and collapses into a strangely reversed world, according to some into a kind of para-universe that exists on the other side of this one. In this respect the passage through this hole is also like the reversal that takes place in Perls' terms when one moves from the implosive into the explosive layer. Some shamans even describe the world on the other side of this one as physically reversed. It is like a journey through the pupil of the eye. In that world left is right, rivers flow backwards to their sources, summer here is winter there. With the guidance of helping or guardian spirits the shaman explores that world carefully and with awe. He never knows what to expect when he learns to "see" in this fashion. It is all "very far out." Whenever he is there, he is completely beyond himself and it is intensely enjoyable. He is ecstatic.

One need not engage in metaphysical argument about the existence or nonexistence of the shaman's other world. Whether it exists or not is not a matter of importance except in the sense that it does already exist Here and Now. It does without question exist in that sense in the world of dreams. Dreams can be experienced not only as enstatic and homeostatic but also as ecstatic. Every night you enter an amazing "other" world, an eternal world beyond time and space. Where are you when you dream and when is it?

As the experience of shamans and other mystics demonstrates, this other world can be cultivated with some patience and care. Several factors are important if you wish to do that. One is *where* you sleep. American Indians often go into the wilderness, perhaps to a sacred place, and spend several days there meditating and concentrating on dreams and visions. If you are not ready for such a venture, try at least sleeping in what for you are wholy places in your house or apartment. Dreams that you have there, like those of Indians on "vision quests," are likely to have special significance. You may also discover that sleeping under a special blanket will help.

As you go to bed, try lying on your back until you are relaxed and ready to go to sleep. If you like, you can turn and lie on your right side with your right hand under your cheek when you are ready to go to sleep. You can also imagine that you are lying with your head on the knees or in the lap of your guru, if you have one either in "real" life or in your dreams. In any case, as you fall asleep, try shutting your eyes, but keep watching the back of your eyelids as if they are a screen upon which a film is about to be projected. This takes a little practice, but you will get accustomed to it easily. Don't try to put anything there. Just watch as you fall asleep and see what happens. You may be surprised. Using this technique, you will be able to "stay awake" as you fall asleep for longer and longer periods of time. Like the shaman you can eventually learn to go where and when you want. In your dreams you have no limits. As you progress with the exercise, you can learn to put the particular place, person, or time that you would like to visit on the screen and keep it there as you fall asleep.

If you do not have any success with this exercise over a period of time, forget about it for a while. It takes a long time to perfect, and there is nothing that you can do to rush the process. This is especially true if major unfinished situations stand in your way. The "same old thing" will always block the door to the new and different. It is nothing, at any rate, to worry about if you don't have instant success. Worry makes for pushing and pulling and will only make matters worse. It is more than likely, however, that you will at least find your dreams richer and more meaningful than before. Of if you usually have difficulty remembering your dreams at all, it will become easier. Be patient with yourself. People who are very goal oriented usually have a difficult time "making it," no matter what they are doing and how they try. With patience, however, you will discover another world in your dreams, and, unlike heaven, you can visit it every night.

Return once more to the mantram OM. This time focus on the last part (oom-m-m). Notice how both your breath and the sound are now leaving you and entering the world around you and becoming part of it. Be sure to let out all of your breath. Notice how you and the mantram touch the surroundings. Notice the sound leaving both your nose and lips. Notice how your lips are pursed, as if to kiss. Use the last sound of the mantram as your kiss to the world. Tune in to the ecstatic Y*ouniverse*.

Go on to the mantram OM MANI PADME HUM and concentrate this time on HUM, which stands for the heart. The heart is the feeling center, the source of the flow that *is* your body. When that movement ceases, you die. Experience the energy, the power of the mantram. Allow to happen what happens.

As a further and more difficult exercise, use the double image on the page following this section as a visual meditation object. Hold the page at arm's length and turn it so that the images are side by side. Then cross your eyes so that you see a double image. This may take some time and practice. When you can do this, overlap the images so that you see three birds instead of four and stare intently at the "middle" bird. Try to focus on it as well as you can. After a while you will see this image pop out at you and appear to hover half way between the page and you. The object that you see is not "really" there. Watch this bird while you are doing other meditation exercises or as an exercise in itself. If you notice eye strain or a headache developing, discontinue the exercise and come back to it later. See what happens.

What people usually see is at least somewhat arbitrary. According to Don Juan, people do not see the marvels of the world of nonordinary reality because their "membership" in the society of customs and conventions has already convinced them of what and how they *should* see. The religions of the East explain that what people normally see is simply a "world of illusions" (*Maya*). In either case, a new world, one that far exceeds that of "normal" perception, waits to be seen.

There are several techniques for developing this kind of seeing. Of particular interest here are some Tibetan Buddhist techniques called "visualization," the careful and deliberate development of the ability to see images in the "mind's eye," so that one can see them even in great detail with the eyes closed. The person can then engage in certain procedures using the images and watch the changes that take place. Enormous amounts of time, even years, are spent in complete seclusion learning to produce these images to the point where they can be seen in the "real" world. The ordinary then becomes the extraordinary.

For at least a small indication of how such exercises work, go back to the spiral image at the beginning of the book and examine it carefully. Try to close your eyes and see how well you can picture it without looking at it. Then open your eyes and check it out. When you realize that you left out some of the details, shut your eyes again and try to see the image with the corrections. Keep opening and closing your eyes until you can produce the image in perfect copy of the original. Then use this image as an object of meditation and keep at it until you can see it for extended periods of time without your attention wandering off to other things. Now do the same thing that you did with the maze exercise in the last section. Let the spiral lead you into itself. And when you get to the center, stare at it and see what happens. Stay with it as long as it remains productive. You may wish to use it as a meditation object as you are falling asleep. See what opens up on the other side of it.

For a more tactile exercise, go outside at night and "feel" the wind. Dress as lightly as possible so that you can feel the wind with as much of your body as possible. After you have become sensitive to the wind, begin to respond to it by humming, as if you are an Aeolian harp or a wind chime. If you like, use the syllable HUM. Develop your own music with the wind. On quiet, less windy occasions, it can be music that is calm and quiet; on windier occasions it can be more forceful. But always stay with the wind.

As in other exercises, once you get used to it, you can do the exercise at any time of the night or day. As a special feature, however, try doing it with a group of people, so that you can set up your own "symphony" of sound—beginning, building to your climax, perhaps, and then dying away at the end into the silence. Do not "force" the music, however, by getting carried away with your own personal idiosyncrasies, for you can ruin it not only for yourself but for the others as well. Make a single piece of music among you. Just go with the wind wherever it takes you, and this will happen by itself.

For a daydreaming kind of visualization exercise, imagine that you are in a space vehicle that is on its way to a new planet that you are going to explore. As you sit at the controls, you notice that everything is functioning well, so you are watching the sights out the windows. Now you can see the planet that you wish to explore far ahead of you, and you pay particular attention to it as you get closer. When you reach the proper distance, you go into orbit around it and make preparations to descend to the planet's surface by means of a "transporter" beam, the controls of which are part of a wrist watch type of device that you wear on your left wrist. The air there is quite safe to breathe, so you won't need to wear a space suit or helmet. The transporter beam is always available to you while you are on the planet, and if you need at any time to return to the ship, all that you have to do is to push the button and return automatically. So you can feel completely safe during the trip. You have a limited amount of time available for your initial excursion, but it is enough to carry out a brief exploration of the terrain and make contact with any conscious life forms that may be there.

When you push the button of the transporter beam, you slowly disappear from the space vehicle and rematerialize on the planet's surface. Explore as much as you can in the time that you have available. Enjoy yourself. Then when you are ready to return to the ship, push the button and return, and then make the return trip to Earth, landing close to where you are doing the exercise. Then wake up.

This is a relatively easy ecstatic exercise, but it is just as productive as more complicated exercises in its own kind of way. If you have trouble with the problem of whether the planet that you visited really exists, remember that many of the Eastern mystics have the same question about the content of their visions. Some consider the visions objective and others subjective. In the end the answer doesn't make all that much difference. What is important is that it is a moment when in some sense you are beyond yourself, a moment when reality becomes extraordinary for you, a moment when you discover something that is new and significant to you, a moment that is intensely enjoyable. Because the exercise probably involved some if not all of these things, it is the opening of a door or gate into the You*niverse*. Gradually you can work your way further and further beyond that door, but what you may discover at the point that is farthest out is the same door that you left, except that it now leads back in. Going and coming become the same thing.

CONCLUSION?

This book has followed a spiral pattern in its structure as well as its content. Each section leads into the next and the last leads all the way round and starts around again on a level somewhat closer to the center. In that connection, the final exercise may raise the question for you of just who you are anyway.

Teilhard de Chardin, the palentologist, discusses the way that the evolutionary process always develops a tightening, a converging (implosion?) of evolutionary lines just prior to every evolutionary breakthrough into a new level of development. He argues that man is developing toward just such an "omega point," that life is now preparing such a supreme, ultimate stage. He points out how with every passing day it becomes more and more difficult to avoid acting collectively.

> Humanity . . . is building its composite brain beneath our eyes. May it not be that tomorrow, through the logical and biological deepening of the movement drawing it together, it will find its *heart*, without which the ultimate wholeness of its powers of unification can never be fully achieved? To put it in other words, must not the constructive developments now taking place . . . in the realm of sight and reason necessarily also penetrate to the sphere of feeling?[1]

Thus Teilhard projects his "organic super-aggregation of souls."

117

It is easy to dismiss him as a dreamy romantic, but his predictions make more, not less, sense as time goes by. Such a Youniversal Self, or Youniversal Community if you prefer, does embody all three of the Youniversals discussed in this book at one and the same time. Each of the Youniversals entails the elimination of the isolated self and a merging with one facet or another of the Youniversal Self. Such a corporate consciousness is a convergence of all three Youniversals. It is a joining (Part I), an emptying (Part II), and a surrendering (Part III) at the same time.

Perhaps such a consciousness is here already. Certain gurus and wise men do appear to have the ability to wander around inside the whole of human consciousness as if it were their own brains or bodies. But it is not necessary to be all that exotic about it. The everyday world is full of reminders that in the end there is no such thing as "individual" existence. What does it really mean, for example, when people from the deep South say "you-all?" Has anyone considered the possibility that it is a form of religious address? Perhaps "you-all" is the name of God.

In some ways using the second person in this book has been frustrating. It would have been better perhaps to be able like Whitman to use the first person singular and expand it until the "I" becomes everything. But the second person has several advantages, too, like being the same word whether singular or plural. "You" has a universality about it that the other pronouns do not, at least in common usage. At the same time, the "you" does become confusing in time. Who are the parties of the dialogue? Who *are* you? Writers usually need to hear what they are

118

writing as much as anyone else. So the writer may at times identify more with the "you" than the "I." At times the writing even seems to come from "another" voice, so that the writer merely writes down what is dictated. Correspondingly, to the extent that writing makes sense to the reader, it comes from a voice that belongs to the reader already. So just as the writer can be "you," the reader can be "I."

A work of art is not the creation of the artist alone; it is something that happens between the artist and the audience. Maybe one reason why the Lone Ranger never takes off his mask is that he is you. Who wrote this book anway? And who is reading it? Every work of art, every word that is spoken, every conscious act becomes at least a small token of how here and there, subject and object, begin to come together. Hopefully, this book has been of some help in bringing about that kind of union.

So (t)here you are. Yourself is (y)ourself.

FOOTNOTES

Part I

[1]The following exercise is an adaptation from one developed by Professor George I. Brown of the University of California, Santa Barbara in his workshops at Esalen Institute.

[2]Jean-Paul Sartre, *Being and Nothingness: An Essay on Phenomenological Ontology*, tr. Hazel Barnes (New York, 1956), pp. 47–70.

[3]John Bleibtrau, *The Parable of the Beast* (New York, 1969), p. 86.

[4]Ram Dass, *Remember, Be Here Now* (New York, 1971), pp. 90–91.

[5]The full title of McLuhan's famous work is: *Understanding Media: The Extensions of Man* (New York, 1965).

[6]Carlos Castaneda, *Journey to Ixtlan: The Lessons of Don Juan* (New York, 1972), p. 43.

[7]James Joyce, *Finnegans Wake*, 1958 Edition with Author's Corrections Incorporated in the Text (New York, 1959), p. 3.

[8]John Blofeld, *The Tantric Mysticism of Tibet: A Practical Guide* (New York, 1970), p. 76.

[9]Mircea Eliade, *Shamanism: Archaic Techniques of Ecstasy*, tr. Willard R. Trask (Princeton, 1972), p. xvii.

[10]Both shamans and gurus are referred to in the masculine rather than the feminine-masculine form used in the rest of the book. This is because the roles have both been male ones historically, and it seems artificial to pretend otherwise

122

when referring to them. The present and future may be another matter.

Part II

[1]Karl H. Pribram, *Languages of the Brain: Experimental Paradoxes and Principles in Neuropsychology* (Englewood Cliffs, N.J., 1972), p. 25.

[2]Lao Tzu, *Tao te Ching*, tr. Gia-Fu Feng and Jane English (New York, 1972), poem 11.

[3]Daisetz T. Suzuki, *Studies in Zen* (New York, 1955), p. 167.

[4]Alan Watts, *Nature, Man and Woman* (New York, 1970), p. 56.

[5]Carlos Castaneda, *A Separate Reality: Further Conversations with Don Juan* (New York, 1971), pp. 266–275.

[6]Walter B. Cannon, *The Wisdom of the Body* (New York, 1963), p. 24.

[7]Maurice Merleau-Ponty, *Phenomenology of Perception*, tr. Colin Smith (New York, 1962), p. 153.

[8]Christmas Humphreys, *Zen Buddhism* (New York, 1970), p. 104.

[9]Gyomay M. Kubose, *Zen Koans* (Chicago, 1973), p. 17.

[10]*Ibid.*, p. 156.

Part III

[1]Gregory Bateson, *Steps to an Ecology of Mind* (New York, 1972), p. 500.

[2]Idries Shah, *The Sufis* (New York, 1964), p. 58.

[3]Frederick Perls, Ralph Hefferline, and Paul Goodman, *Gestalt Therapy: Excitement and Growth in the Human Personality* (New York, 1951), p. 128.

123

[4] Frederick Perls, *Ego, Hunger and Aggression* (New York, 1969), p. 102.

[5] *The Collected Poems of William Butler Yeats* (New York, 1956), p. 293.

[6] *Tao te Ching,* poem 76.

[7] Frederick Perls, *Gestalt Therapy Verbatim* (Lafayette, Calif., 1969), pp. 55–57.

[8] Eliade, p. 4.

Conclusion?

[1] Pierre Teilhard de Chardin, *The Future of Man,* tr. Norman Denny (New York, 1964), pp. 177–178.

BIBLIOGRAPHY

Bateson, Gregory. *Steps to an Ecology of Mind.* New York, 1972.

Bleibtrau, John. *The Parable of the Beast.* New York, 1969.

Blofeld, John. *The Tantric Mysticism of Tibet: A Practical Guide.* New York, 1970.

Cannon, Walter B. *The Wisdom of the Body.* New York, 1963.

Castaneda, Carlos. *A Separate Reality: Further Conversations with Don Juan.* New York, 1971.

_____. *Journey to Ixtlan: The Lessons of Don Juan.* New York, 1972.

Eliade, Mircea. *Shamanism: Archaic Techniques of Ecstasy.* Tr. Willard R. Trask. Princeton, 1972.

Humphreys, Christmas. *Zen Buddhism.* New York, 1970.

Joyce, James. *Finnegans Wake.* 1958 Edition with Author's Corrections Incorporated in the Text. New York, 1959.

Kubose, Gyomay M. *Zen Koans.* Chicago, 1973.

Lao Tzu. *Tao te Ching.* Tr. Gia-Fu Feng and Jane English. New York, 1972.

McLuhan, Marshall. *Understanding Media: The Extensions of Man.* New York, 1965.

Merleau-Ponty, Maurice. *Phenomenology of Perception.* Tr. Colin Smith. New York, 1962.

Perls, Frederick. *Ego, Hunger and Aggression.* New York, 1969

_____. *Gestalt Therapy Verbatim.* Lafayette, Calif., 1969.

_____, Ralph Hefferline and Paul Goodman. *Gestalt Therapy: Excitement and Growth in the Human Personality.* New York, 1951.

Pribram, Karl. *Languages of the Brain: Experimental Paradoxes and Principles in Neuropsychology.* Englewood Cliffs, N.J., 1971.

Ram Dass. *Remember, Be Here Now.* New York, 1971.

Sartre, Jean-Paul. *Being and Nothingness: An Essay on Phenomenological Ontology.* Tr. Hazel Barnes. New York, 1956.

Shah, Idries. *The Sufis.* New York, 1964.

Suzuki, Daisetz T. *Studies in Zen.* New York, 1955.

Teilhard de Chardin, Pierre. *The Future of Man.* Tr. Norman Denny. New York, 1964.

Watts, Alan. *Nature, Man and Woman.* New York, 1970.

Yeats, William Butler. *The Collected Poems of William Butler Yeats.* New York, 1956.